GRUMPY OLD ROCK STAR

GRUMPY OLD ROCK STAR

AND OTHER WONDROUS STORIES

By Rick Wakeman

with Martin Roach

preface
publishing

Published by Preface 2008

10 9 8 7 6 5 4 3 2 1

First published in Great Britain in 2008 by Preface
1 Queen Anne's Gate
London SW1H 9BT

An imprint of The Random House Group

www.rbooks.co.uk
www.prefacepublishing.co.uk

Addresses for companies within The Random House Group Limited
can be found at www.randomhouse.co.uk

The Random House Group Limited Reg. No. 954009

A CIP catalogue record for this book is available from the British Library

ISBN Hardback 978 1 84809 004 0
ISBN Trade Paperback 978 1 84809 068 2

The Random House Group Limited supports The Forest Stewardship Council (FSC),
the leading international forest certification organisation. All our titles that are
printed on Greenpeace-approved FSC-certified paper carry the FSC logo.
Our paper procurement policy can be found at www.rbooks.co.uk/environment

Mixed Sources
Product group from well-managed
forests and other controlled sources
www.fsc.org Cert no. TT-COC-2139
© 1996 Forest Stewardship Council
FSC

Typeset in Fairfield by Palimpsest Book Production Ltd,
Grangemouth, Stirlingshire
Printed and bound in Great Britain
by Clays Ltd, St Ives PLC

CONTENTS

I actually consider myself extremely fortunate to still be alive after all I've been through (well at the time of writing this dedication in June 2008 I was still alive anyway), and therefore be able to share some of my tales of the 'unexpected', 'inexplicable' and 'unbelievable' adventures as both a musician and a grumpy old man.

So many of my musician friends that I grew up with and worked alongside are sadly no longer with us, and so it is to all of them that I dedicate this book, as in their own way, they have all contributed greatly to my becoming a Grumpy Old Rock Star, of which I am immensely proud!

INTRODUCTION

Simple maths . . .

On the day this book is published I will have been a professional musician for forty years.

People who know me well, know that nothing 'ordinary' ever happens to me and a 'Spinal Tap' tale of one sort or another will always seem to come about whether I am on the road touring, in the studio recording or just simply walking down the road!

So where does the maths come into it?

Well working on the very conservative estimate that at least three ludicrous things happen to me every year, then a simple calculation will tell you that at least 120 completely farcical events have happened in my life since 1968.

Work backwards through my semi-pro years, college and my schooldays and you've just added at least another hundred such stories.

Therefore, the final maths sum will tell you that potentially, this book is the first of a possible twenty volume set.

I never did like maths much.

MY LIFE AS
A RUSSIAN DOLL

You know those Russian dolls, the ones that are made to fit inside each other? Well, I was one of those once.

Funnily enough, it was in Russia.

Music has gifted me the opportunity to travel all over the world – touring with Yes, taking my own solo shows around the globe, promotional trips abroad, it's a lot of air miles. And I've come back with as many bizarre experiences as I have souvenirs. On one occasion it was the souvenir itself that put me in a very peculiar situation indeed.

I was booked to do a TV show in Moscow, deep behind the Iron Curtain. The trip was right in the middle of the Cold War, and East/West relations were not good. I'd travelled there before and loved the country – I used to come home with my suitcase crammed full of souvenirs. With $20 in cash, you could buy the world. The kids and family all loved the red T-shirts with the hammer and sickle on them, the woolly fur hats . . . standard tourist fayre.

Luckily, the customs officers at the airport tended to turn a blind eye to all this black-market stuff.

Apart from the KGB uniform I bought from a total stranger in a dark alleyway.

What's all this got to do with a Russian doll, you say? Bear with me . . .

My hotel was typical of the type used by Westerners. Police guards on the main doors and barricades outside. You were told there were places you could go, places you couldn't, things you could do, things you couldn't. Admittedly, it could be quite difficult because the British and American politicians didn't trust the Russians and the Russian politicians didn't trust the British or Americans.

I loved the Russians and got on with them great. The TV show went very well and myself and the band had a lovely time. It was only after the filming that things started to get complicated.

It was no secret that the Russian black market couldn't get enough dollars. The buck could buy you anything, and I mean *anything*! Funnily enough, the dollar bills themselves had to be crease-free, in absolute mint condition. They also needed to be low denominations, one or two dollars ideally.

This one particular day I slipped a dollar into the hand of the policeman on guard at the door of my hotel and went off wandering. It was *freezing*, properly cold. I was wearing this absolutely huge coat I'd bought in America which was like a rancher's coat – it was massive. As I trotted off down the street, I looked like Mr Blobby crossed with J. R. Ewing. Any Westerners wandering around certain dingy backstreet lanes were so easy to spot and with my hair, height and rancher's coat I was like a beacon of the West crunching loudly through the snow. It wasn't long before I was approached by a very suspicious-looking character who'd clearly bought his battered old brown suitcase from Arthur Daley or Del Boy Trotter. Most of these characters actually knew me because, as I've said, I'd been over a few times and was always a willing customer. You'd walk along a main street and from the shadows of a dark alley you'd hear, 'Mr Wakeman, over here, you buy T-shirt?' These 'entrepreneurs' would then open some dusty old suitcase and offer you perhaps five T-shirts for a dollar. They weren't exactly the finest quality but I always bought quite a few and enjoyed our little chats.

However, on this occasion, it wasn't a paper-thin T-shirt that I was offered.

It was a genuine KGB uniform.

Out of a suitcase.

From a complete stranger down a back alley, off the beaten track in the middle of Cold War-entrenched Moscow.

Don't ask me why, but when this man whispered for me to go down this shadowy dead end to look at what would obviously be illegal merchandise, for some reason unknown to my right-thinking mind I did. He huddled behind a wall and opened up his case, saying, 'Here, KGB uniform. Is good.'

I knew this was playing with fire. Being in possession of a KGB artefact or uniform was considered a very serious crime.

I knew all of this.

However, it was a really very splendid uniform.

Splendid.

At first I assumed it was a fake and I told him so. He was having none of it.

'No, really, this is KGB. My brother's uniform. I got hat too.'

'But how do I know it's real?'

'It was my brother's. He was in KGB and then . . . he . . . er . . . left.'

'Right. And how the hell am I supposed to get this thing back to my hotel room?'

'You take off big coat, put on KGB uniform underneath, put big coat over top and put hat in bag – nobody know.'

'How much?'

'Five dollar.'

'Done.'

I took off my *Dallas* coat, furtively changed into this long KGB greatcoat and, with my fingers struggling to grasp the buttons in the cold, put my own coat over the top. Looking like a blimp, I started to walk away, back towards the main road.

'Mr Wakeman . . .' It was the same guy, shuffling after me.

'What?'

'You want to buy admiral's jacket?'

Great. I couldn't resist.

He opened up his case again.

'It's splendid, very nice. How do I know it's real?'

'Is really real, this is actual admiral jacket. It was my other brother. He was an admiral and then . . . er . . . he wasn't.'

'You've got a lot of family in the military, haven't you?'

'Er, yes, well, er, I did have.'

'Right, and how do you suggest I get this back to the hotel as well?'

'Is easy. You take off coat, put admiral's jacket over KGB one of my other brother, then put your coat over top.'

At least I wasn't going to be cold.

He took this admiral's uniform out of his suitcase and it really was beautiful, resplendent with these magnificent shiny buttons and badges. Every bone in my body was telling me I was sailing a little too close to the wind, but it certainly was a splendid uniform.

'How much?'

'Eight dollar.'

'Done.'

By the time I'd got changed again I made Pavarotti look like Twiggy. I could barely walk down the alleyway without turning sideways. I'm thinking, *This is absolutely preposterous*. I got back to the hotel and the guard on the door just laughed out loud when he saw me. I slipped him a dollar and he didn't care any more. He just carried on chuckling as this six-foot-plus multi-layered Russian doll with blond hair waddled across the foyer.

Sweating and rather breathless, I got back to my room and peeled off all these layers, then laid the two uniforms neatly out on the bed, next to the dolls and T-shirts I'd also ended up buying. The uniforms were really very splendid. However, scary visions of decades of hard labour in a Siberian prison camp were giving me severe doubts about the wisdom of trying to smuggle these things out of the country. I felt lucky not to have got caught wearing them in the street and I was just anxious to get back home. So, despite the absolute logic of my sensible purchasing decision, it was with a heavy heart that I decided to leave the uniforms behind.

At this point the phone rang. It was someone from the TV company; they still had our passports, which needed exit visas stamped in them. Bloody visas. Me and visas have never really got on very well, but I'll tell you more about that later. As soon as I heard his voice, I thought to myself, *Please don't let there be a problem with the visas.*

'Mr Wakeman, I'm sorry but there is a problem with the visas.'

Great.

'But I have been assured that the visas will be ready for your Aeroflot flight home in the morning.'

I put the phone down and started to head off for some food but, with my anxiety levels escalating, I turned back to my bed and carefully folded the uniforms up in my suitcase. Then, just in case a maid – or someone else – came into my room while I was away, I locked the case and hid it under the bed. Best to play safe.

The next morning there was no sign of the passports at the hotel. I called the TV company and they assured me that the visas would be waiting for me at the airport. By now I was in a right state – all I wanted to do was go home, all I could think about was my passport, my exit visa and how I desperately did not want to miss my flight. I headed off to the airport with hours to spare.

Back in those days, Russian airports were like some throwback to a railway station in the 1920s, and the ticket desks were just little wooden holes in the wall with pale undernourished faces behind them. Very few Russians flew so these decrepit buildings were often a hive of Westerners. I explained my situation and that I had been assured the passports plus visas would be waiting for us in time for our flight.

No sign of the passports.

Great.

I sat down on this old wooden bench with the rest of the band while people made enquiries. There were no telephones, we didn't know anyone and our flight-departure time was getting worryingly close. My mind was a whirl with what to do about these visas. We sat there for an eternity . . . but no news.

Then our flight left.

Without us on board.

Just after we realised the plane had gone, a sternly dressed man in a dark suit walked over to me. Without introduction he said, 'Mr Wakeman, can you come with me, please?'

Of course, I complied and followed him into this tiny office. He was Head of Security at the airport. In the corner was a little cabinet with a very old kettle on it, next to a small table – not even as big as a desk – and his chair to one side. We could barely both fit in the room. It smelled musty and very 1950s. He introduced himself as Igor – I kid you not – with a second name I couldn't understand but it did end in 'kov', and said, 'Sit, please, sit. Mr Wakeman, you did not go when your plane left. Why is this?'

I said that we didn't have our passports or visas and explained at length all the problems we'd had. He said there was an unscheduled British Airways flight stopping at the airport that afternoon and he could arrange to get us on that. He took the phone number of the TV station that had our passports and said he would make some calls and get the visas sorted. Then he instructed me to buy these new plane tickets while I waited. I was sent to some Finnish airline with an even smaller office. Bizarrely, they accepted my AmEx card and gave me four scraps of paper that looked like old betting slips but were, apparently, plane tickets. When I looked at my credit card receipt . . . it was for $2,000! This was a small fortune back then, but by this stage I didn't care.

When I got back to Igor's office he was on the phone to the TV company; he appeared to be quite irate with them and had explained that I was now $2,000 down because of their problems with the visas. The TV guy came on the phone, apologised profusely and said, 'I have your passports and I have your visas. I come over now. I will bring $2,000 in an envelope for you to airport . . .'

'No! You can't do that – I'm supposed to leave the country with the same currency I came in with. That's worth about a billion roubles . . . they'll never let me out.' By this point, I was waiting for novelist Len Deighton's spy character Harry Palmer to walk through the door. Or Michael Caine, who played Palmer in the movies.

The passports finally arrived with visas stamped in them. Igor was visibly relieved and he said to me, 'OK, I think everything sorted. Tickets, passports, visa . . . I will offer my help to get you through customs quick but you need to tell me if you have like Russian dolls or any T-shirts, that kind of thing. Do you have anything that you shouldn't have in the suitcase, Mr Wakeman?'

It was at this point that, for the very first time that day, I realised that in my rush to get to the airport I hadn't taken out the KGB and Soviet admiral uniforms, which were folded neatly in the suitcase that nestled between my legs, next to Igor's table, in that small 1970s office, in that decrepit airport, in Cold War Russia, thousands of miles from home.

'Er, yes, well, there are a couple of little things, yes.'

'OK, what like, dolls, yes? You like Russian dolls?'

'Er, no.'

Igor opened the suitcase and looked in. His face went as white as the snow that was tumbling onto the tundra outside.

'Mr Wakeman, what is this?'

'It's an authentic KGB uniform, I believe.'

'Yes, I know it is KGB uniform, Mr Wakeman, but what is it doing here?'

'It's a cracking uniform,' I offered, clawing for some hope.

'Is not possible, Mr Wakeman. No one has those uniforms.'

'But they are real, they belonged to this chap's brother . . . er . . . and he was in the KGB and . . . er . . . then he left.'

Igor leaned across the table and said, 'Rick, *nobody* leaves KGB.' He put the tips of his fingers in a pyramid of anxiety and sat thinking for a few moments. Then he said, 'OK, here is what we do. I may be able to help you but you must help me, Rick.'

At that moment, I could think of very little I wouldn't do to 'help' him – I could almost smell the gruel they served at the Siberian labour camp.

'Anything, sir, I'll do anything. What is it you want?'

'Some records by Led Zeppelin. And The Who, yes?'

I don't think I've ever been so relieved in my life. I was in a very serious situation and yet here was something so trivial and easy for me to get hold of that could remedy everything.

'My friend, I can get you records by anybody you like!'

'Even The Yes?'

'Yes, even The Yes.'

He quietly explained that Lufthansa trucks were able to travel across East/West borders relatively unchecked and that was how we would be able to get him the records. I promised him I would send all the records he wanted and he hastily scribbled out a list. He then escorted me to the metal detector at customs and whispered in my ear, 'Do not worry, Rick, KGB long coat is just cloth, it will not set off metal detector.'

'No, it won't, sir, but the badges and buttons on the admiral's uniform in there might.'

He went white again.

'Not possible, Rick. How? Wait, let me guess: same man?'

'Same man. His other brother. He was an admiral and then . . . er . . . he wasn't.'

'I see. Follow me.'

It couldn't get much worse.

But it did.

As we were walking across the airport with these two highly illegal uniforms in a case that was about to be smuggled through customs by a security man from the KGB himself, a man from the TV company came running across and said, 'Rick, Rick, I have your passports and visas and I have got your $2,000!!! I am good man, I make my word, Rick!!!' and promptly handed me a huge brown-paper bag stuffed full of one- and two-dollar bills.

Quick as a flash, Igor said, 'Hide it.'

I had to think fast. I looked at my three travelling companions from the band and they were like, 'We're having nothing to do with this!' so I stuffed the money down my pants and into my socks.

Best I could do.

When I looked up, the customs officers were just standing there across the hall, watching me.

I have to tell you, laugh as I might now, I was shitting myself.

Then, like a dead man walking, I trudged up to the customs desk. I handed them my ticket, exit visa and passport. The guy started to grumble something but then Igor took him into a little booth and whispered something in his ear. The customs man came back and waved me and my contraband suitcase straight through, unchecked.

Next up was the currency desk where they examined your money. Including, in my case, $2,000 from a brown-paper envelope shoved down my pants. I looked up – and I mean up – at a woman who made Giant Haystacks look feminine. She said, 'You came in with $100 and £130 sterling and you changed £30 into roubles and so you need to leave with £100 sterling and $100. Or do you have any other currency on your person that you wish to tell me about?'

I was standing there, literally bloated with dollar bills rammed down every crevice and the odd orifice. Two minutes earlier, she'd watched me stuff all this money into my trousers.

'Er, no, no.'

Cue Igor and his little whisper in the ear and, once again, I was waved through. Within five minutes I was sitting on a virtually empty plane, struggling to fit into the seat with all these dollars spilling out of my pockets and more intimate regions of my trousers. After a few minutes, a stewardess came over to me and said, 'We are actually only here for refuelling, Mr Wakeman, we are not supposed to take passengers on board here. I've heard you had some fun and games – you must have a story to tell . . .'

'Yes, you could say that. And one day I might be able to tell it.'

EVER BEEN CONNED?

Long before KGB uniforms, TV shows in Russia, before Yes, before touring the world, prog rock and all that jazz, I was just a kid who loved music and playing the piano. As Louis Armstrong once said, 'It's a wonderful world,' but for a naive sixteen-year-old trying to break through into the music business in the 1960s I don't think he was referring to the wonderful world of showbiz management.

At that age you have so much to learn.

Here's one of my very first lessons – how I met, worked for and subsequently wasn't paid by one of the greatest music-biz managers of all time.

In the mid-1960s radio was in the grip of a so-called 'non-needle time' controversy. With the explosion of vinyl sales and the prevalence of records rather than live tunes being played on the radio, the Musicians' Union were very worried that musicians were being forced out of work. They campaigned vehemently against this and, consequently, it was agreed that on Radio 1 there had to be a certain amount of what was christened 'non-needle time' – namely the broadcast of live bands rather than just vinyl. It's absolutely true, strange as it may seem now. DJs like Jimmy Young (who I think is about 128 now) would play the hits of the day and, every now and then, would have to throw in a live track. To be fair, although it sounds archaic now the practical reality was that this regulation did indeed create work for live musicians.

One of the most renowned 'non-needle time' artists was a great singer called James Royal. He was managed by Mr Mervyn Conn who, sadly, is no longer with us. To this day, Mervyn's moniker remains the most appropriate I've ever come across in the business.

Mervyn Conn . . . because so many of us were conned.

Despite this apparent managerial handicap, James Royal had made himself one of the most used non-needle-time artists around; it got to the point where James Royal and the Royal Set were getting more phone-in requests than artists with big record deals. I later found out that a large majority of these fan letters came from James's mum. She lived in south Ealing but wrote dozens of letters to the BBC – to avoid suspicion, she first mailed these letters to her friends around the country who posted them in from distant addresses to avoid detection. Before long, between his mum and the large amount of genuine fan mail and requests he received, James Royal was the most requested person on the radio anywhere in the world.

Where did I fit into all this and how did my path cross with that of Mervyn Conn?

Well, my path to James Royal's door came via the Red Lion pub in Brentford, a great, old-school rock 'n' roll pub where musicians from all over the place used to congregate and jam together on a Thursday and Friday night. Loads of amazing players, like John Entwistle (from The Who) and James Royal. For me, as a sixteen-year-old hopeful, it was an incredible privilege to play alongside the likes of these people. I used to go down there in my mate's battered old Land Rover with my battered old

Hammond in the back and spend all night playing with these big-name session musicians. I just loved it.

James Royal was a really nice guy and I was very flattered one day when he said, 'Would you like to come in and play a Radio 1 session with me?'

I nearly fell over in shock.

'And here's a list of the session guys who'll be playing with you . . .'

It was just about every top name I admired.

'And you'll get paid £2 a session.'

I was in heaven. You could fill your car up with petrol in those days for £1.

When the day came I made my way excitedly to the old underground Maida Vale Studios in London which were made famous during the Second World War. It was a fantastic little labyrinth, with a tiny control booth and recording room. They recorded each live session direct onto quarter-inch tape – there was no mixing, it was done as quick as that. I say 'live', they would actually bring in about half a dozen musicians who'd play together for around three hours, performances which were recorded and then used for the non-needle time. For some reason, there was always a woman sitting in the corner knitting. With cotton wool stuffed in her ears.

Later, I asked why she was there and it turned out that her presence was a throwback to the war. Apparently, during the conflict there had been a shortage of skilled producers and technicians, largely because they were all being killed in action, I suppose. So the BBC had brought in a lot of women to do what had previously been seen as 'men's jobs'. These women were given permanent contracts so after the war finished the BBC had little choice but to keep them on. These old women would sit in the corner of the studio with their ears blocked against the 'noise' of the band . . . and knit.

Anyway, my first session went very well and, thankfully, James was really pleased with my playing. I was delighted to be asked back and before I could catch my breath I'd done six weeks of sessions. I couldn't believe my luck. It was great fun.

Then I realised that I hadn't yet been paid. I broached the subject with James and he told me that his manager looked after that side of things.

It was time to go and meet Mervyn Conn.

His office was up near Leicester Square, so I filled up my little Ford Anglia – you'll learn more about this legendary automobile later – and drove to London for the very first time. I shat myself – I'd never seen so much traffic in my life and had no idea where I was going. Although I only lived five miles or so outside London, it was in a quiet leafy suburb surrounded by fields and it might as well have been another planet. I vividly remember heading along the A40, my mind a blur, as the chaos of the city enveloped me.

Somehow, I eventually found Mervyn Conn's office, right in the middle of the West End. I walked up to the door which had a little sign bearing the inscription – no word of a lie – 'Mervyn Conn Artists'. At the top of a very narrow staircase there was a small reception area with a girl sitting behind a desk.

I nervously said, 'I've come to see Mr Conn. I'm Ricky Wakeman.' (People used to call me Ricky in those days. An early girlfriend said it sounded more American and cool because Richard sounded like an old fart's name. Perhaps I should be called Richard again now?)

So . . .

'What band are you from?'

'James Royal and the Royal Set.'

She went through a door to her left and closed it behind her. Then I heard her say, 'I've got a Rocky Wigwam outside, says he wants to see you.'

'Send him in.'

I was very nervous as I sat down opposite Mervyn Conn. He was sitting behind an enormous old oak desk, flanked by four walls crammed with gold discs. I remember thinking to myself, *Wow! I've hit the big time!* He was very friendly.

'I've heard all about you, Rocky.'

'Er, it's Ricky, Mr Conn.'

'Yes, I've heard all about you, Ricky.' He clearly hadn't got a bloody clue who I was or why I was there. 'I've heard all about what a great player you are.'

'Thank you, Mr Conn.'

'James speaks very highly of you and tells me you are one of the country's best young guitar players.'

'I play the organ, Mr Conn.'

'Yes, one of the country's best young organ players.'

'I've been told to come here to collect my session wages. Six sessions at £2 a session which makes £12, Mr Conn.'

'They are fabulous sessions, aren't they? Very popular too, you know . . .'

I just kept saying 'Yes' and 'Thank you very much' to pretty much anything that came out of Mervyn Conn's mouth. He kept talking and then suddenly stood up from behind his gigantic desk. Automatically, I stood up too. Mervyn was smaller than I thought, so when he came around by my side he had to reach up to put his arm round my shoulder. He slowly walked me to the door and said, 'You have a great, great future, Rocky . . .'

'Ricky.'

'Yes, a great, great future, Ricky. From what I hear, you are going to be up there with all the big names.'

'Thank you, Mr Conn.'

As we stood in reception next to the girl on the front desk, he took my hand in both of his and said, 'Any time you need to chat to me, you know where I am, come and see me.'

Then he turned, walked through into his office and shut the door.

I smiled at the girl, delighted by how well the meeting had gone, and made my way down the narrow staircase. I strolled to my car and, just as I was getting in, thought, *I haven't got my money!* I walked back up the street, back to the office door, up the narrow staircase and into reception.

'Can I see Mr Conn again, please?' I said.

'I'm afraid he's gone out to a meeting.'

I'd literally been out of the office for thirty seconds.

'When will he be back, please?'

'In a week.'

'Oh. So how can I get hold of him?'

'Just give him a ring.'

I rang for weeks and weeks but never got through.

Mervyn Conn.

I never got paid.

I took a view on it: I was young, inexperienced and here was a chance to play sessions for the BBC with some of the world's top players. The £12 would have been wonderful but I still thought I was doing well.

Years later, I bumped into James and we were laughing about Mervyn and the non-needle-time days. These revered veterans had a genuine affection for those days and felt privileged to have learned so much from them.

'You know, James, I never got paid . . .'

'You know what, Rick? Nobody did!'

How did a sixteen-year-old come to be playing in a pub with some of the country's best musicians, you ask? It is a tawdry tale of crap equipment, a riot and an alcoholic baptism of fire, so bear with me . . .

By the time I was getting 'paid' work from Mervyn Conn I was already the veteran of several working bands. Let me tell you first about the fabulously titled Atlantic Blues. Back when I first started, being a pianist posed a practical problem for simple monetary reasons. You could pick up a guitar for about a fiver, but a little electronic piano would set you back about £50 or £60. Given that the average weekly wage was about £14, and my pocket money was 25p in today's money, this was an astronomical cost. Also, there was no affordable or readily available form of amplification for electronic pianos, so even if you did save up for one the chances were that no one would be able to hear you anyway. The practical repercussion of all these problems was that you ended up making do by playing old-fashioned acoustic pianos.

Quite often, the line-up of a band was decided more by what gear someone owned than by their actual musical ability. For years, it was said that Bill Wyman first joined the Rolling Stones because he had more equipment than the rest of them. Ken Holden from the Atlantic Blues was the same, although that's where the similarities between us and the Stones ended. Ken was, by his own admittance, a pretty inadequate drummer behind a full kit, yet oddly, due to him being in the Boys' Brigade, he was a brilliant snare drummer. He was aware of this foible and even tried to make up a kit out of a Boys' Brigade snare and a bass drum, but he only had one cymbal. Then he upped the ante by purchasing a Gigster drum kit – it only cost £12 from Woolworth's and was the cheapest, nastiest, flimsiest kit imaginable. It was so weak that when you hit the foot pedal the bass drum actually went completely oval. On average it took just over twelve seconds to assemble. I believe they are quite valuable nowadays because so many of them didn't last. Back then, they were shambolically poor but *it was a kit* so Ken was suddenly in demand. Ken was very like Keith Moon – not in terms of his drumming ability, God no, but due to the fact that he was totally unaware of anything else going on around him.

19

Then he pulled a masterstroke.

He bought a van.

Never mind: do you want to be in the band? If you had a van, it *was* your band!

With Ken's friend Derek on bass guitar, myself on piano, Ken on drums and a really good rock 'n' roll guitarist called Alan Leander, we formed the Atlantic Blues in 1963. Ken painted our name down the side of his battered old van and we were in business. We even had a manager, Paul Sutton, also a member of the Boys' Brigade, aged thirteen. We rehearsed in the Civil Defence Hall in Northolt Park, which was great fun. No one could afford proper amps but fortunately Ken worked as an electrician for London Transport and was a bit of an electronics wizard. He bought a broken old Vortexian amplifier for £1 and somehow fixed it, even wiring up three inputs – the distortion was horrendous and actually only one of the three inputs could really be heard . . . we didn't care, we had an amp! They hung a mike by my piano so I was *virtually* amplified; Alan had loaned Ken the £1 to buy the amp so, in return, it was Alan who always got the 'loud' socket.

Basically, all you could hear was Alan Leander.

But we had a lot of fun.

The Atlantic Blues was a great period for me. We rehearsed regularly and in no time at all had progressed from being very poor in performance to just plain poor.

Then Ken came to us one day and said, 'We've got a gig!' We could have fallen through the floor. Back then it was everybody's dream to get a proper gig – the kudos was enormous. Many of the pubs in the area had live music. My local was called the Timber Carriage, which was on the A40 at Northolt and it was perhaps most famous for having entertained the Soviet Premier Kosygin when he needed to urinate as his cavalcade drove past one time. Legend has it that he insisted on using the toilet in the public bar – someone apparently overheard him saying it was the loo that the proletarians used. Within twelve hours of said communist urine hitting said democratic porcelain, there was a plaque over the urinal in question reading, 'President Kosygin pissed here', along with the date and exact time. It's a McDonald's now. They didn't keep the plaque up.

A little further down the A40 towards Hayes, there was another pub which had a hall at the side with a stage where they used to put on pop-and-rock nights, and one time the Atlantic Blues was given a slot supporting a rock band from France. We were fed up playing the Civil Defence Hall on our own, so this was welcome news. I cannot tell you how excited we were.

The other band arrived and we were gobsmacked, because they had *an amplifier each*, which was unheard of. The drum kit must have had twenty-three cymbals – Ken still only had one. We were informed that we'd have to play for half an hour, that we would not be getting paid but if we went down well we could be looking at a rebooking and then maybe get a fiver between us. I was even more excited now, with the prospect of being paid to play in the future.

Then I looked around the hall.

There was no piano on the stage.

'Where's the piano?' I asked, not unreasonably.

'It's down there,' said the landlord, pointing to the other end of the hall.

Sure enough, the piano was situated against a wall at the other end of the hall. We started trying to move it but the landlord stopped us, saying there wasn't enough room on the stage and it had to stay there, take it or leave it. I was keen to play whatever the circumstances, so I left it at that.

There was a bit of a strange atmosphere in there, that night. When our slot came I duly walked down the back of the hall and sat at this lonely upright piano, with 150 people between me and the stage. The band started playing and I couldn't hear

21

a bloody thing, Ken's timing was all over the place, no one could hear me and it was a disaster.

Then the most amazing fight broke out.

In the crowd between me and the band.

I carried on for a few bars, trying to peer over the fists and broken bottles of this fairly violent skirmish, but soon realised it was actually quite a dangerous situation and, besides, no one seemed to be listening. Almost in synch, the band gave up playing and fled for the nearest exit they could find, carrying their precious gear with them. We all dived into the van and sped off before the police arrived to break up the brawl – which turned out to be a clash between two rival local gangs.

Alan Leander was gutted and said, 'What a complete waste of time!'

'Oh, I don't know,' said Ken, holding up a very expensive pair of cymbals belonging to the headlining rock band, 'We appear to have three cymbals now!'

After a rather strange residency at a social club for people with mental disorders – don't ask – I joined a local dance-band quartet which did a lot of work for weddings and other family events. It was proper money, £3 a night – bear in mind that when you are at school and the average pocket money is half a crown, £3 is serious dosh. And this outfit worked three nights a week, mainly over the weekend. It was an unusual line-up – guitar, drums, piano and clarinet – but people didn't mind in those days.

This latest band was called the Concorde Quartet and the first problem was that, until I joined, it was a trio. It was run by a guy called Bernie Vick, a drummer in his early twenties who lived with his mum and dad in South Harrow. He worked for Boosey & Hawkes, which meant he had access to very cheap sheet music, which was great; plus the work was generally very local, with a lot of the functions being at Ealing Borough Social Club.

Apparently, their previous piano player had got pissed every night. This was fine for the first hour or so, but many of these functions lasted four or five hours with only a few short breaks. It wasn't ideal that the piano player was paralytic and couldn't play even before the buffet had been served; worse still if, by the cake-cutting, he was trying to shag the bride. I believe this sort of problem let to his demise.

The first gig was down at the Tithe Barn pub in South Harrow. I was fourteen, and I'd never actually been in a pub before, not for a drink anyway. However, I was already six foot two and looked older than my years, so this wasn't a problem. There was a public bar, a saloon bar and a lounge bar which also went out into a ballroom. If you wanted to hear some music, you paid an extra penny with your pint and went into the lounge bar.

We started the show at the Tithe Barn and it was going down a treat. There were guys in there singing loudly and making requests and I was having a great time. Every now and then, someone would put their pint on my piano and go and have a dance.

After about an hour, Bernie said, 'Thank you, ladies and gentlemen, we're going to take a break now. We'll see you in fifteen minutes for some more music.' Then he turned to my piano, pointed at the collection of full pint glasses and said, 'Rick, my friend, you'd better get through some of these, they ain't half mounting up . . .'

What?

It turned out that the regulars were in the habit of buying drinks for the band and leaving them on the piano top – so within sixty minutes I had four pints to get through. By the time I drank them, they'd been replaced by three more and a couple of Scotches. I started drinking the spirits after that, because the sheer volume of the beer was killing me.

At the end of the night I got on my bicycle to ride home.

I couldn't feel my head, legs or arms. Or stomach. Or feet. Or hands. I just had this warm glow all over my body. But apart from that I was as sober as a judge.

Using the strange logic of a drunkard, I decided to cycle through the park, figuring that would be safer than using the roads. At the end of the park, the path took a ninety-degree turn to the left, as straight on was the local allotment.

I managed to get most of my bike out of the allotment, but not all of it.

I carried the remains of my bike the rest of my way home.

I got blind drunk for the next two weekends, just the same. With my bicycle out of action, one of the band kindly took me home in his car. My mum, bless her, had absolutely no idea about me being drunk. She just thought I was 'very, very tired', and even said to my father, 'It's really taking it out of him, playing these shows and going to school.'

Sure enough, it was hard work and with each subsequent drinking session I was taking a dreadful hangover with me to school every Monday morning.

Where I was in joint charge of the tuck shop.

The 'shop' was actually a big temporary hut in the middle of the playing field and all it sold was crisps and Coca-Cola. The kid I ran it with, an Irish fellow, came up with a brilliant wheeze using a bottle of Scotch. He worked out that if he took the caps off the old-style Coca-Cola bottles, there was just enough room to pour some Scotch in. These were known as 'Specials', cost nine pence instead of the usual sixpence and were only meant to be sold to the sixth-formers. We used to go in early, get all the caps off, and pour the Scotch in ahead of the queues forming, so no teachers would know.

Which was great, as long as me and this Irish fella were working the tuck shop.

However, one day we were hauled up for some misdemeanour

that I can't recall and they had to get someone else in to run the tuck shop.

Someone who didn't know about the Scotch.

Someone who served all the eleven-year-olds first.

With the Specials.

In the middle of the morning.

The first eleven-year-old to puke was taken along to the medical room. 'Probably got a tummy bug, little dear.'

The next two were also taken along to the medical room, with a few raised eyebrows on the foreheads of the teachers. By the time there were sixty first-year pupils puking and stumbling around like drunken tramps, our moonshine scheme was rumbled.

They never managed to pin it on us, but we were both taken off tuck-shop duty.

Meanwhile, back with the Concorde Quartet business was booming. It was a little odd for me to be playing so much dance music: I still wanted to play rock 'n' roll but there was no income in that – I'd been with the band for two years by 1965 and all the money was made playing in the dance bands. There were still social clubs everywhere and at weddings people wanted a live band and to sing along to the old band tunes. People were still dancing waltzes, foxtrots and quicksteps, they were still doing that more than rock 'n' roll. We would often throw in a 'pop' slot, where we'd do pretty ordinary covers of the latest pop tunes of the day, but it was mainly older stuff.

We got ourselves a really good reputation and even started working abroad . . . well, by 'abroad' I mean as far out as Southall. That was quite a few miles out of our patch and with the cars at our disposal and the appallingly small and slow road network, such as it was back then, we might as well have been playing in Germany.

We played some amazing shows but none more so than a wedding at the Hayes British Legion. Funnily enough, I was already starting to think about leaving as I'd had enough of playing the dance music. The venue told us that they had their own piano, which wasn't unusual – although it often transpired that any 'house piano' was wildly out of tune. I quickly learned to walk into any venue, open the piano lid and hit an 'A', while Terry Beresford would play a 'B' on his clarinet, which sounded like an 'A', and see how far we were out of tune.

We walked into the Hayes British Legion and there in the corner was a crisp white upright piano. I was immediately impressed. The rest of the band started getting their instruments out and setting up, so I walked over to the piano to hit an 'A' for them to tune up, which they did. The wedding party arrived and the best man announced that the bride and groom would start off the dancing, which was my cue to play the intro for 'The Lady is a Tramp'. Terry counted me in and I hit the keys – and the only sound that came out was this wooden thumping noise. Terry looked over and beckoned for me to try again, which I did, with the same result. I lifted the lid of the piano and peered in. There was only one hammer in the whole bloody thing. The 'A'.

We went and found the caretaker who was, for some reason, immediately belligerent.

'What's the matter?' he said, frowning.

'Well, it's the piano . . .'

'What's wrong with the bloody piano? I saw it painted with a fresh coat of white myself just last week. It's spotless.'

'Yes, it is very lovely to look at. But it has only got one hammer.'

'Listen, I don't want any crap from you lot . . .'

I spent the rest of the evening getting pissed with the brides-maids.

'BRUDDY HELL,
THEY DONE IT AGAIN!'

Those few pints on my piano as a sixteen-year-old evolved over the course of the next two decades into one of the most savage drinking habits in the music business. During that time, I joined and left Yes and started my own solo career, but I'll come to that.

First, let me tell you about my involvement with the English Rock Ensemble – possibly one of the hardest-drinking bands ever to grace the stage. Made up of some of the finest musicians I knew, we toured the world and in the process I enjoyed some of the most memorable times of my life.

And several I can't remember.

We drank a plane dry on the way to Japan once.

Back in the early 1970s, there were not that many direct flights to Japan. You would normally stop off somewhere like Moscow or Anchorage, when all the passengers had to get off while they refuelled the plane.

On this particular flight, we were heading out to play with the Tokyo Symphony Orchestra. The band and crew boarded this jumbo to find it was half empty – I'd say there were no more than a hundred people on board.

It was a fair few hours to our refuelling stop at Anchorage, so we all had a drink, naturally. There were about twenty of us in the entourage and remember, this was a huge drinking band, *massive*. We drank all the European beer, moved on to the Japanese beer and drank that, then we polished off the spirits, the small bottles of wine and finally the sake.

When we were still about an hour out of refuelling at Anchorage the steward came up my aisle.

'Mr Rakeman, the captain has informed me, is dlink all gone. No more.'

'Really? Not even sherry or perhaps a glass of port?'

'Is all gone, Mr Rakeman.'

He then informed me that the plane's food and beverages would be restocked along with the fuel in Anchorage. I have to say at this point that the lads in the English Rock Ensemble were always very well behaved – they might have drunk like fish but they were always on their best behaviour. Anyway, we landed and headed off to the Anchorage terminal, which in those days resembled a giant tin hut with a model of an enormous grizzly bear outside. We located the bar within seconds and ordered drinks. We sank a few more rounds and, when the time came, we reboarded the plane and settled down for the final leg to Tokyo. We called the same steward and placed orders for yet more drinks.

And then some more . . .

When we were about an hour out of Anchorage the steward came sheepishly back up to my seat again.

'Mr Rakeman.'

'Yes, how are you doing?'

'Velly well, Mr Rakeman, but the captain has informed me, is no more again. All gone.'

It was unbelievable, we were laughing so much, we'd drunk the plane dry twice on one journey. The stewards were lovely and we all had a good old giggle about it together.

We duly landed, disembarked and headed off to the Hilton Hotel, where all the bands stayed, thinking nothing more of it.

The promoter in Tokyo was a man called Mr Udo who, I believe, is still big news in that country's music business even though he must be well into his seventies by now. He's one of the loveliest men you could ever meet. He met us off the plane – 'Herro, Lick!' – and we followed his car to the hotel. We were all really knackered but we headed straight to the bar for a final few jars before retiring to bed.

The next morning, Mr Udo was there to meet me at the hotel. The plan had been for him to talk me through the schedule for rehearsals, the set-up of the orchestra, the various protocols and so on. Instead, looking rather shell-shocked and holding up the front page of the biggest newspaper in Japan, he said, 'Lick, it says here, you dlunk the prane dly . . . twice.'

Obviously I couldn't read the Japanese script so he read out the article in all its hilarious detail. So now I knew the Japanese for 'European beer, Japanese beer, spirits, small bottles of wine and sake'.

'Er, is this a bad thing?'

'It says the steward says you velly nice people, velly well behaved but he never see anything rike it in his rife!'

'OK, but is it a problem . . . ?'

'Not a ploblem for me, Lick. Japanese Airlines, they rish to sponsor tour!'

The actual shows themselves were magnificent. Until our arrival in Japan they hadn't quite sold out but within hours of the newspaper headline about drinking the plane dry you couldn't get a ticket for any money. I believe it was the first time anybody in Japan had a show sponsored, as it was pretty unheard of back in the mid-70s, so that all helped too. The show was a huge hit on both nights and a thoroughly enjoyable experience. On the first night we initially played stuff from my 1973 solo album *The Six*

Wives of Henry VIII, then after the interval we played the whole of my 1974 solo opus *Journey to the Centre of the Earth*, which had been a Number 1 record in Japan (no dinosaurs this time, but we'll come to that . . . all will be explained).

The audience were fantastic. They seemed to take to me and part of that was my size – most Japanese people are fairly modest in stature whereas I am six foot two and a half in my bare feet and had all this long blond hair, so whenever I walked along a Japanese street I'd be bobbing up and down miles above the crowds. I was seen as quite a novelty, really.

Our rider for the shows was thirteen pages long; side after side was like a brewery stocktake: beers, wines, spirits, every drink imaginable. Then, on the very last page, there was a small gap and a single line for the food order, which read 'Salted peanuts – but not crucial'.

We always used to get through our rider, what with the thirst of the band and crew, but also all our guests who we liked to entertain at each show. During the interval for this first night in Tokyo we noticed there were a dozen bottles of very expensive champagne on top of our requested rider. We thought nothing of it, assuming that Mr Udo had sent them as a welcome gesture. We left them where they were and got stuck into the rider, quickly polishing off these vast quantities of alcohol between us. Then my tour manager, the immortal Funky Fat Fred (you'll meet him properly later on), came in and said there was a technical fault with the miking up of the violins and that there would be a half-hour delay before we could resume. We were a little pissed off because it was such a great buzz and we didn't want to disappoint the crowd, but it was explained to us that Japanese crowds were exquisitely well behaved in every respect and there would not be any problems as a result of the unforeseen delay. Naturally, to while away the time we turned to the only alcohol left in the dressing room that lay untouched, those mysterious dozen bottles of champagne. There were seven of us in there and the twelve bottles went down very nicely indeed.

Eventually, the technical faults were fixed and we went back on to play *Journey* and the remainder of the show – it was *fabulous*. In the dressing room afterwards there was such a buzz – we were all talking about the symphony orchestra, the crowd, the emotions were hard to put into words. At that moment there didn't feel like there was a high in the world to come close to it. Amazing.

Then the door opened.

It was my tour manager, chaperoning a gaggle of about ten very senior Japanese businessmen in tailored suits into the dressing room.

Now, I love the Japanese, their culture is so respectful and I love all the very particular etiquette that they observe. The Japanese ooze respect, which makes you more respectful back; I think that a lot of the Western world has lost that element of consideration whereas the Japanese have always retained it in their culture. To me it is like an incredible breath of fresh air every time I visit there. One trick I had learned from the few occasions that Yes had played over there was that when a businessman gives you his card, you don't do what we do in Europe – namely pretend to look at it for half a second and then shove it in your pocket. You should read it very carefully in front of that person, bow and thank them. The first man gave me his card and I dutifully read it: he was the most senior executive at Japanese Airlines.

He proceeded to introduce me to all the other board members of Japanese Airlines, who all gave me their cards, bowed and paid me their respects. After much bowing and thanking, the head executive stepped forward again and said, 'I velly much hope you enjoy show, and as a token of appleciation, we sent twelve bottres of champagne to dlink with you, Lick.' He turned to the dozen now-empty bottles of champagne strewn across the table and said . . .

'Bruddy hell, they done it again!'

Our drinking wasn't always to our benefit, naturally. Roger Hodgson, my percussion player, had a serious bladder problem; he was probably the biggest drinker by far, outrageous, but he couldn't really hold his water much more than an hour and a half max, which was unfortunate as our set was three hours long. So he came up with this ingenious solution of hanging a bucket on his vibraphone, which he would endeavour to pee into during the loud sections of the show. Every now and then his timing wasn't great so I'd be starting a very delicate piano piece only to hear the sound of a man pissing in a fire bucket.

In the end, the crew complained that although they didn't mind lugging the gear, climbing up precarious lighting rigs and working eighteen-hour days, when it came to the crunch they were not paid to empty Hodgy's pisspot. I said, 'Well, someone's got to do it,' but they were having none of it; by way of making their point they drilled holes in the bottom of his bucket. So the next time he played his shoes got rather wet.

My wonderful but, sadly, late trumpet player Martin Shields was also a quite marvellous and phenomenal drinker. He was also a fabulous trumpet player. Of course, these two attributes don't always work together too well. For one, you need firm lips for playing a trumpet and on more than one occasion when he'd sunk a load of booze he'd play like a cross between the theme tune for *Coronation Street* and a Salvation Army band. Then he'd fall asleep and start snoring.

One particular night in America with the English Rock Ensemble, Martin had had an absolute skinful. How he even stayed standing was beyond me. You always knew how far gone

Martin was from the amount of vibrato in his playing. Unfortunately, on this particular evening there was a *lot* of vibrato. He still sounded great, though, and he always looked the dog's bollocks, draped in a white satin suit. The band looked impressive too – we lined up in a very unusual way with the drummer at one end of the stage, effectively with everyone in a straight line and me on a rostrum behind them. It was very dramatic.

The very last part of the title track, 'Journey . . .', finished on a top 'D' for Martin, which was technically pretty impressive. It's a good note, top-of-the-range stuff. Now, Martin could hit this note no problem when he hadn't had a drink; like I said, he was a quality trumpet player. However, he was so remarkably drunk this night I thought there was no way he was going to get this note.

Martin didn't share my pessimism.

He thought he could do it.

As the note approached, I looked at him and he was totally focused on reaching this top 'D'.

It came to the final chord and I saw his cheeks tighten and he went for it . . .

. . . He hit the top 'D' . . .

. . . And shat himself violently.

I watched in stunned amazement as the rear of Martin's pristine white suit turned into what could only be described as an Ordnance Survey map of a sewage farm in Watford. To put it politely, it stank.

The band very quickly cottoned on to what had happened and without a word between them they all moved away, up to the other end of the stage by the drummer, leaving Martin all on his own. The audience were completely bewildered as to why the band were cramming themselves into one corner of the stage while the trumpet player stood alone on the opposite side. I had to say something.

'I expect you are all wondering why the band are all down there. It's because Martin has shit himself.'

The crowd all started laughing because – obviously – they thought it was a joke. Martin was horrified, however. He turned around to face me and said, 'Oh, don't tell them that!' – in the process revealing the full extent of the stains on his white suit. The audience let out a communal 'Urgh!!!'

With my own rampant drinking through the 1970s and 1980s, I did not escape without my own fair share of embarrassing drink-induced incidents. So pour yourself a glass and let me tell you about two particularly memorable moments.

The year is 1973. I was still in Yes – just – but had already released my first solo album, *The Six Wives of Henry VIII*, which was critically lambasted on its initial release. The music press had slated it and no one else seemed interested. This frosty media reception obviously made it very hard to maintain a good profile and promotion on the record – the music journos had made their minds up and they slaughtered it.

So when my record-company A&R man of the time, Tony Burdfield from A&M, burst into the room and said, 'Rick, I've got you on *The Old Grey Whistle Test*,' this was very big news. For starters, this was to be my first major television appearance. It was filmed down at the BBC – you recorded the music quite early in the afternoon and then headed off for a break, before coming back to do the interview live with the renowned presenter, 'Whispering' Bob Harris.

I'd got a band together and we were well prepared. On the day, we performed immaculate renditions of 'Catherine Howard' and 'Catherine Parr' after which the production staff told me I wasn't needed until much later that night. So off I trotted to the now-defunct BBC bar. I was a serial drinker at this point, but I knew this *Whistle Test* interview was really important so I resolved not to get drunk. The *Whistle Test* never had huge viewing figures but as a programme it was taken very seriously. This was my chance to reignite interest in *The Six Wives of Henry VIII*, so I couldn't take any chances.

Unfortunately, in the bar I met up with an old friend who was also a serial drinker. Suffice to say, despite my best intentions, when the production girl came to get me, I'd been drinking heavily for five hours and I was completely paralytic. I must have downed half a bottle of Scotch and several bottles of wine. I can recall this girl apologising for the delay in getting me to the studio for the live interview, at which point I stood up . . . but not for long, as my legs had gone.

I staggered to the door, my head was throbbing and I was just thinking, *I've blown it*. The programme director, Mike Appleton, came over to me and immediately realised I was completely pissed. With admirably quick thinking, he said, 'Right, Bob's very good and he's going to keep this interview short – he's just going to ask you three questions, Rick. Keep your answers short. He's going to ask you how long it took to record the album, then who played on the album and finally if you are likely to tour the record.'

As he was talking to me, I was plodding through his words in my brain, processing them syllable by syllable in drunken slow motion . . . *Right, how long it took to record the album? . . . It took nearly a year . . . Who played on the album? . . . Right, Chris Squire, Bill Bruford, Steve Howe . . . And are we likely to tour? . . . Unlikely because of commitments with Yes . . . We're all right here, Rick, you can do this . . .*

Whispering Bob Harris sat me down in front of the camera and started to ask the questions, just like I'd been told.

'Well, Rick, tell me, who played on the album?'

'A year.'

Bob just looked at me and quickly decided to plough on.

35

'Er, right. So how long did it take you to record this album, Rick?'

'No, we probably won't be touring it, because of Yes commitments.'

Again, a brief silence before the final question.

'Right . . . and tell me, are you likely to tour the record?'

'Chris Squire, Bill Bruford, Steve Howe.'

At this point, the camera panned back in a near-panic and it was all over.

In the end, they cleverly used two of my replies but re-edited it to save my blushes.

Or, perhaps, theirs.

I was delighted to find out some years later that this particular edition of *Whistle Test* had actually enjoyed some of the programme's best-ever viewing figures, way more than the normal ratings. There was a reason for this and, if I'm being honest, it wasn't my odd, drunken interview.

The same night, the highly controversial Andy Warhol film *Blue Movie* was due to be broadcast on BBC1. There had been uproar about this film. Mary Whitehouse was in a state and it was in all the papers and on radio. People were up in arms about whether the BBC should be showing this apparently morally degrading film. Of course, all this actually meant was that *everyone* knew about it and *everyone* wanted to watch it. It was television's must-see movie of the year.

The Warhol film was due on just after 11 p.m., so most people were planning to leave the pub before closing time and head home to watch it, myself included. I got back to my house in Gerrards Cross and switched on the telly, only to be met by an announcement that the BBC were no longer able to show the Warhol film. Now, this was in the days long before a thousand satellite channels – you had BBC1, BBC2 and ITV. That was your lot. It was too late to go back to the pub, so I resigned myself to staying in and flicked over to ITV to see what was on there. That was rubbish so, in desperation, I tuned in to BBC2. Across the nation, millions of disappointed people were doing exactly the same thing at the same time, flicking on to BBC2.

And what did the nation find on that oft-ignored channel?

Yes, my stupendous, drunken interview with Whispering Bob Harris on *The Old Grey Whistle Test*.

The following week, *The Six Wives of Henry VIII* flew up the charts and went on to sell millions of copies all over the world. I've got Andy Warhol to thank for that.

And so we come to my second example of the drink causing a stink. Good old Radio Solent. The early days of commercial radio were as limited in many ways as the formative times in television. While your TV set only picked up three channels, your choice of radio listening was only slightly more expansive. There just weren't that many commercial stations about. You had your local BBC stations but commercial ones were few and far between. For an artist like me, who at that time was considered prog rock and unfashionable, getting radio was always difficult. Most prog-rock shows were either on late at night or didn't exist at all. Strangely, this made prog-rock followers even more elitist about their music but from an artist's point of view it meant a lot of hard work travelling around to these fledgling commercial radios doing interviews and trying to increase your radio air-time somehow.

Down in Portsmouth, they had Radio Solent.

I'm banned from there, you know.

Over something and nothing, a few naughty words, a few glasses of port and brandy.

They banned me for life.

A guy called Dave Christian ran the station. He'd previously been a Radio Luxembourg stalwart and he was a really nice guy.

They had a midnight rock show and kindly invited me to go on there to talk about and play some tracks from my 1975 solo epic *The Myths and Legends of King Arthur and the Knights of the Round Table*. That record is a whole other chapter, but let me tell you about Radio Solent first.

I travelled down there first thing in the morning because I wanted to pay a visit to an aunt and uncle I had living in Portsmouth. After I'd seen them, I headed off to the radio station but it was still only lunchtime, so I took a detour into the pub a few doors down. I made friends with the landlord, sank a few pints, had a bite to eat, found the dartboard and had an altogether very pleasant afternoon until they closed at three.

In the early evening, I went round to the radio station and met a really young kid who presented the midnight rock show. We chatted about all sorts and he obviously loved music. His job was to come in just before the rock show started and turn off the pre-recorded tapes of a gardening show that was on at 11 p.m. He explained that, late at night, the station wasn't manned by anyone else and by the time the show started there'd only be myself and him in the building.

'Do you fancy a pint and a sandwich next door?' I asked.

'Ah, well, I shouldn't really, I'm not really a drinker . . .'

I think he came out of some sense of duty. After a couple of rounds, I asked him if he'd ever drunk port and brandy. Perhaps not altogether surprisingly, he hadn't.

'I'll buy you one.'

By eleven-fifteen, it really was time to get back to the station and, besides, it was throwing-out time.

Or in the case of the young engineer, throwing-up time.

As the landlord shouted, 'Time, gentlemen, please!' across the pub, this kid stood up and then fell flat on his face across the table. Poleaxed, he was. Paralytic, unconscious. With the help of the land-lord, I manhandled him into the radio station and poured coffee and water down his neck for twenty minutes. He was incapable of doing anything.

I finally roused him so he was at least conscious and tumbled him into this tiny studio. I tried to fix his glazed eyes and said, 'Listen, don't worry, we'll play *King Arthur*, it's a long record, we can just play it all the way through and you can get some more coffee.'

'I feel sick . . .' came the less-than-encouraging reply.

As it turned out, we never got as far as being able to play my record. When the gardening programme was coming to a close he was supposed to start the rock programme. He took the mike, and then, live on glorious Radio Solent – 'The Sound of the Solent', no less – he made his considered announcement.

'Fuck gardening, does anyone actually listen to that shit? This is Rick Wakeman's *King Arthur* and it's much better.'

He tried vainly to put the needle on the record but it just jumped wildly, scratched loudly and then leapt to halfway through the first side shortly before he returned to his previous state of unconsciousness.

Within seconds, the phone-in indicators on the control desk in the studio had lit up like a Christmas tree.

There wasn't much I could do, really, so I sat there and waited for the inevitable. Sure enough, about fifteen minutes later Dave Christian stormed into the building, shouting – furious he was.

The following day Tony Burdfield rang me from his office at A&M Records.

'Rick, can't you go anywhere?'

'Oh, come on, Tony, it really wasn't that bad . . .'

'Rick, he didn't say "bum". He said "fuck" and "shit" live on air.'

To be fair, this was 1975, it was pretty unheard of. When the Sex Pistols did it two years later on Bill Grundy's television show, they became national hate figures. My fate was far worse.

I got banned from Radio Solent for life.

I wrote Dave Christian a long letter explaining that it was totally my fault, that the kid hadn't really wanted to go for a drink but was just doing what he thought was the right thing for the station, entertaining a guest and all that, that he was in among serious drinking company and should be absolutely exonerated. Rather than sacking him, they transferred him to another station.

About ten years later, I was invited down to Radio Solent – which by now had changed hands – to do a quiz in aid of Children in Need. I hadn't even got through the main door when I was met by this security man, looking rather embarrassed.

'I'm sorry, Mr Wakeman, there's been some kind of mix-up. It has become apparent that a few years ago you were banned from Radio Solent for life. The directors have had a meeting and decided to uphold that ban.'

'Are you serious? I'm here to support Children in Need – you are having me on, aren't you?'

'No. I'm sorry, Mr Wakeman.'

So they wouldn't let me in.

Not even for Children in Need.

The Sound of the Solent, eh?

I can't believe anyone would be so petty, all those years later. But judging by the number of places that still uphold life bans against me, which include Julie's Restaurant in Notting Hill Gate and the Roof Gardens in Kensington, then it's not surprising really!

'HELP YOURSELF, TUCK IN'

Rewind a year and life for me back in the Yes camp was good. No lifetime bans from Radio Solent, for a start. I'd joined in 1971 and that year we'd released the acclaimed album *Fragile*, followed the next year by *Close to the Edge*. I was working with technically gifted musicians, touring the world and selling millions of records. We were a huge band with massive record sales. Our live shows were constant sell-outs and, without being immodest, we really were a very large band.

The interesting thing about Yes was that it was completely different people who all had their very strong, good points and conversely also had some quite unbelievably bad points – myself most definitely included. We were all entirely different. That dynamic was kind of essential to our chemistry.

Take vegetables, for example.

And meat.

Or in the case of most of Yes, the lack of meat.

I liked to eat meat. The rest of the band were vegetarians. Also, they didn't drink – although rumour had it that one or two indulged in the odd substance here and there. So I was a little bit of a fish out of water, to some extent. I was the steak-eating heavy drinker. Meat seven times a week, please.

Nowadays, I'm the only teetotaller and eat meat no more than three times a week.

To be fair, Steve Howe doesn't drink much – the odd glass of wine – but the rest all like a drink. And they are all now confirmed carnivores, again with the exception of Steve (who has stuck by his position all these years and I take my hat off to him). So there has been a complete reversal of roles.

Before I go on, I'd like to mention one thing that I've never understood about vegetarianism. I have no objections to it at all, but what I don't understand is if you don't like meat, why do you make things like nut cutlets to look like a chop? And tofu to look like sausages or burgers? I've never understood that.

I digress.

On Yes tours, food was constantly a hot potato, on the menu, dish of the day – you take your pick of clichés. For one tour, it was decided that we would take a chef on the road with us. I wasn't surprised, as we'd pretty much taken everything else we needed over the years, so why not a chef?! Some of the band were quite extreme with their vegetarianism. For a couple of Yes, having a meal with no meat in it was not enough; they had to know pretty much the origin of the soil it was planted in, the organic farming methods used in its production, the name of the guy who planted this food and, ideally, the species and health of the birds who had shit on the organic soil where these plants and vegetables were grown. Well, that might be possible in the noughties in an organic wholefood specialist shop; but try this in a Holiday Inn coffee shop in the Deep South in the early 1970s. Some of the band were going without food for days and it was becoming impossible.

So our manager, Brian 'Deal-a-Day' Lane, called a meeting at his Notting Hill Gate office. We looked at the reality of the band members' food preferences and, of course, the only way around this was to take a chef on the road.

Yes was never really blessed with management who knew how to handle the band. However, in all fairness, I'm not sure that Yes were 'handle-able', because none of us would take advice. Whatever meeting we were in, whatever advice we were given, we would all just sit there and listen patiently, then go out and do whatever we wanted. Which was invariably a disaster.

So that's what we did in this case. We decided to hire a chef for the tour. In between mouthfuls of sirloin, I remonstrated.

'Hang on, guys, I have absolutely no objections to getting a chef. I accept you have strong principles and a chef will accommodate that. What I don't accept is that this chef isn't going to come cheap and, what's more, we are going to need to take a kitchen on the road with us too. Now, no disrespect to you guys, but I don't think I should pay one fifth of these costs.'

They said that I could eat their vegetarian food too, if that helped.

Perfectly reasonably, I said, 'I do not want to have an organically reared nut cutlet in the evening for the whole tour with a lettuce leaf that has been washed on the banks of the River Nile by a spiritual woman's feet . . . or something. I really don't want to know.'

At this point, Deal-a-Day stepped in and suggested that the chef could cook separate meat-crammed meals for me. This seemed like a fair compromise and, on reflection, I actually liked the idea of having these delicious meals made for me – after all, tour grub is pretty lousy and I do like my food.

So we hired this fabulous English chef and he flew out to America with us for the tour. He had all the top professional stoves and an amazing amount of equipment. Basically, what happened was this: at each hotel, we rented a small reception room, laid the table out and then at the end of each show we would go back to this room and all sit round and eat, including the management and any other members of the tour party.

Very early on the first day I'd chatted with the chef about what he was going to cook for me. I was actually very interested by now and glad we'd taken him along. I just agreed to eat whatever vegetables he was cooking for the rest of the band, and he said he'd stick a bit of steak or chops in for me too, in a separate pan. This all worked out very nicely.

Then, on the first Saturday of the tour, this chef took me to one side and said, 'Rick, do you fancy a nice big roast tomorrow?'

'Bloody hell, do I fancy a roast!'

'Well, I haven't asked before because there's no point cooking a roast for one person, but I understand your manager will be eating with us and your accountant David Moss, and neither of them are veggies. What do you think?'

'Absolutely.'

'Right, Rick, I'll go out today and buy a smashing turkey with all the trimmings.'

I was beginning to think that taking a chef out on tour was a stroke of genius.

We played the Sunday show and I headed back to the hotel virtually floating on saliva at the prospect of this roast. We all sat down and the chef brought out the rest of the band's food first: a lettuce leaf, a carrot or two, celery sticks, whatever . . . and they all tucked in, giving it the old rather unconvincing 'mmmm' and 'delicious'.

Then he walked out, went back to the kitchen and a minute later banged back through the door with an enormous silver platter on which sat a 22 lb turkey, golden brown, heaped high with sausages wrapped in bacon, potatoes and parsnips. It was a sensational sight.

The veggies around the table stopped eating, some of them with forks halfway to their mouths.

Jon said, 'What's that?'

'It's a roast turkey, Jon.'

'Yes, I know it's a roast turkey, Rick, but what is it doing here?'

The chef, meanwhile, put the roast in front of me and started serving it up; the smell was incredible.

Someone said, 'Er, could I try some roasted parsnips, please?'

'Sorry, chaps, cooked in goose fat.'

'And the potatoes . . . ?'

'Goose fat. Rick, shall I cut the breast or the leg, sir?'

I could barely pick my plate up, there was that much roast turkey piled onto it. With the exception of Steve, I think every veggie around the table watched every mouthful go in. Steve never batted an eyelid, but the rest were struggling badly. After they'd all finished their veggie meals a mass exodus ensued, clearly to avoid being around this delightful roast for too long.

A few minutes later I still hadn't finished and was just heaping some more sausages wrapped in bacon on my plate when the door opened. It was Alan.

'All right, Rick. I was thinking, I know I'm veggie and all that, but to be honest, I do eat the occasional piece of white meat. Any chance I could try some of the turkey?'

'Alan, of course you can – tuck in, help yourself,' I said.

'OK, thanks, but I'll take it back to my room, if that's OK.'

He hastily put some of the roast turkey and trimmings on a plate and off he scurried.

Five minutes later, the door opened and Jon walked in.

'All right, Rick. I was thinking, I do have the odd bit of chicken now and then, so I was wondering . . .'

'Help yourself, tuck in, Jon,' I offered.

'Cheers, Rick. I'll take it back to my room, though, if you don't mind.'

Ten minutes later, door opens, Chris walks in.

'All right, Rick . . . I, er . . .'

'Help yourself.'

I turned to the chef who was grinning widely. 'Probably best if you don't mention this, my friend . . .'

Fast-forward to 2003, and Yes were playing some overseas shows. We were at an airport eating rubbish departure-lounge snacks and I had opted for a sweaty cheese sandwich. I think it was Alan who said, 'That's funny, Rick, you're eating cheese and, apart from Steve, we're all eating meat. That reminds me, do you remember the time you had the chef make you a roast-turkey dinner in the States . . . ?'

I smiled knowingly, in between mouthfuls of cheese.

People often wondered what planet the various members of Yes were on. Some even suggested that we regularly visited other planets to get our music. And clothes. And hair. And stage sets. I'd like to think that Yes was a pioneering band, I don't think that's unreasonable. Especially in the early days with regards to some of the stuff we did onstage. Take a look at *Spinal Tap* — we did that stuff for real.

During the *Tales from Topographic Oceans* album project, the grandiose elements of Yes were spiralling out of all control. I have to be honest and say that was not my favourite Yes album and I said so at the time. We'd ended up with too much material for a single album but clearly not enough quality songs to genuinely fill a double album. This was 1973, way before the days of CDs, which was a shame because we could have used just the good songs and fitted them on a CD nicely. Don't get me wrong, that album had a few really nice songs and melodies on it, but basically it didn't work for me personally. It felt like the record had been stretched a little thin.

Maturely, I renamed the album *Tales from Toby's Graphic Go-Kart*.

We took the album out on tour and the stage set was unbelievable. We'd been using Roger Dean for the artwork and he'd become like a sixth member of the band. Yes was always a very visual band and by this point, the sets we used were colossal. Again, if you've seen *Spinal Tap* you'll know what I am talking about. There is a scene in that film where the bass player is trapped in a giant pod – well, that *actually* happened to Alan one night. He was placed with his drum kit inside a giant seashell pod, it was truly enormous. However, when it came time to open, the gearing jammed and he was trapped inside.

The problem was, it was a sealed unit, so Alan quickly began to run out of air.

This was onstage, live, with thousands of people watching.

You could almost hear him clawing for breath.

Suddenly there was a real dilemma. How on earth were we going to finish the song properly with no drums?

The roadies started trying to smash the pod open, all the time staying out of the line of sight of the crowd so that no one noticed. That wasn't working so they got some oxygen pumps and tried that and eventually, somehow, they prised this bloody thing open with pickaxes. The audience must have noticed the rescue effort because as the pod sprang open a huge cheer went up, and Alan stumbled about gasping for breath.

The sheer scale of the stage sets that Yes used was breathtaking. Sometimes I needed directions to get to my keyboards. If satnav had been invented, it would have been very useful. Sometimes I felt like I was journeying through the Himalayas. 'Yes, take a left here, Rick, climb over that giant mushroom, past the seashell and the spaceship and just behind that, beyond that cloud, are your keyboards.'

This was the same for all of us and it was generally fine when you played a conventional stage, facing the audience. But when we started to perform 'in the round' – where a circular stage is planted smack bang in the middle of the venue with the audience circling the band 360 degrees – getting to our instruments was suddenly a major headache.

I think it was Jon who suggested a solution and said that he thought it was a bloody good idea. He said, 'We need a tunnel, then we can all get to the stage in one piece and quickly.'

'We can't dig a bloody tunnel under the floor of every venue, Jon!' I pointed out, not unreasonably.

'No, Rick, we build an *overground* tunnel, and it will look fantastic.'

He was right.

It was a bloody good idea.

We had this immense tunnel built out of what appeared to be very strong rice paper. It looked like the world's biggest Chinese lantern. Using the finest engineering science known to man, we based it on the Slinky, you know, those toys that flip down stairs. The tunnel folded in on itself for shipping and opened up into great elongated hollow paper worm for the show each night. We ran lights through the inside and it looked absolutely brilliant. As the music started to play, we'd walk through the tunnel and our silhouettes would alert the audience to our presence, raising the tension – it was amazing.

The crew hated it.

And as any seasoned rock musician knows, if the crew hate something then that something will eventually stop being used.

They hated it because the paper would rip, the wooden frames would split, it never folded in on itself as easily and neatly as they'd want, it took too long to work and it was almost impossible to cart around. So they made their feelings known and, respectfully, we completely ignored them.

After losing yet another particularly heated argument about this problem, at the very next show the crew took their revenge. Unbeknown to us, they redirected the tunnels away from the stage.

The music duly started and we all strode excitedly along inside the illuminated tunnel, only half noticing that the sound of the audience was getting further and further away, until we finally came to a halt by a large green EXIT sign.

We didn't use the tunnel again.

DRINK LIKE A FISH,
SMOKE LIKE A CHIMNEY

Back then I never would have imagined that by the 21st century I would be spending a large amount of my leisure time gardening, but it is certainly better for your health than the lifestyle I have led for much of my time on God's green earth. By the late 1960s, I was a prolific drinker. By 1971, when I first joined Yes, I was quite an accomplished alcoholic. I was really very, very good at it. I never indulged in any other substances, but alcohol was a speciality of mine.

Then, in 1975, I nearly died.

I'd already recorded *Journey to the Centre of the Earth* as a solo project and I was very excited about it; conversely, I wasn't enjoying what was happening in Yes. That band was always at its best when you contributed a lot as you then received a lot back in return.

Earlier on, I certainly felt I was putting in my fair share, sometimes more on occasion, but that was no problem because it was reciprocated, I was getting a lot out of it. However, by this stage, due to circumstances and the musical direction in which we were heading, there was increasingly less and less I could put in and it was becoming very unrewarding. The management knew I was unhappy and after I told them in January that I wanted to leave they reassured me that, once the heavy touring schedule was completed and we could start rehearsing the new material, it would all be fine.

'No, it won't.'

'It'll be fine, Rick, it'll be fine.'

I knew my time in Yes was nearing its end.

I couldn't handle it any more.

Rehearsals were due to start on 18 May 1975 – I know the date because it was my birthday. I used to have a farmhouse down in Devon and I'd gone down there to clear my head. It was a very weird day. First off, I got a phone call from the Yes management asking why I wasn't at rehearsals that had started that morning.

'I told you back in January, that's it, I'm off. I don't want to do this free-form jazz, I can't contribute anything to it, it's not me and I don't think it's Yes.'

They tried to talk me into rehearsing but my mind was made up; then they asked if I would kindly not tell anyone until they had found a replacement. Five minutes later the phone rang and it was Terry O'Neil from A&M Records in London. He sounded ecstatic.

'Rick! I've got some amazing news! *Journey* has just gone to Number 1 in the album charts!'

'Has it? Great.'

'Well, you don't sound very bloody pleased – we're all going nuts up here, it's the first Number 1 the label's had in the UK and we're all getting pissed.'

'Sorry, Terry, I've had a weird day, it's my birthday and you've just told me that news about *Journey*, but five minutes ago I officially left Yes. But you must not tell anyone.'

'Shit.'

You may recall that while I was drinking that plane dry in Japan my 1974 solo album *Journey to the Centre of the Earth* had hit Number 1 in that country and several others. With it topping the charts in the UK too, there was even less reason to stay in a band that I wasn't enjoying.

Long before Yes rehearsals started, I'd booked the enormous Crystal Palace to put on an extravagant live show for *Journey*. When I say 'extravagant', I mean it. Fifty-piece orchestras were no longer enough for me, huge stage sets didn't cut it, this time I also had . . . dinosaurs.

But we'll come to that finally, dinosaurs and all. Bear with me . . .

The *Journey* show at Crystal Palace was booked for the summer and I started rehearsing like crazy. I was drinking phenomenally heavily and I used to smoke far too many cigarettes as well. I wasn't exactly a party animal, out with all the latest pop stars, it was more like old-fashioned excess. I was a pub man: beer and skittles, darts and dominoes. Nonetheless, regardless of whether I was in a pub or at home or in the studio, my excess was reaching frightening levels.

And, it turned out, very dangerous ones.

The problem was that I was very much burning the candle at both ends.

And in the middle.

I would rehearse in the day, then head off to the studio and work there until really late, and after that I'd head out to a lock-in at a local pub till four or five in the morning. Then it would all start again at eight or nine the next day. Then add to that an increasing amount of pre-publicity for the shows and writing and yet more rehearsals, plus meetings about the stage set and the show itself – not forgetting my chronically wayward lifestyle – and basically you had a recipe for disaster. I think that for many weeks I was surviving on adrenalin only.

On the day at Crystal Palace, the situation started to get dangerous. I had a beautiful black and silver left-hand-drive Mustang, with a huge great V8 engine that made the most wonderful noise. I drove that to get to the show but I felt ill all the way there – or rather, I started feeling *numb*. What I mean by that is, say for example when you've had too much to drink and your head has a certain type of numbness . . . well, my entire body felt like that.

I got to Crystal Palace and parked up the car. By the stage were some tents and the support acts had already started playing. Then I saw Tony Burdfield and Terry O'Neil from A&M Records and they came over to talk to me, but I couldn't concentrate on what they were saying. I wasn't pissed – because I'd felt ill previously I'd only drunk a fraction of my usual consumption. Yet Terry and Tony were saying things to me and I couldn't really follow, there was this fog across my brain, almost like I was in a different world. I came onstage with the New World Symphony Orchestra and English Chamber Choir and we played the show. But from a musical point of view, I just remember it was incredibly hard to concentrate on the pieces, the notes, the timing, everything.

It was a real struggle. In that state, you tend to do a lot of things on autopilot and that was certainly the case that day – I was not on top of my game at all. I had to think about every single note and it was exhausting. Going back for an encore pretty much finished me off. Afterwards, I slouched offstage and sat down, whereupon I think I fell asleep for a little bit. I now felt very, very numb and I remember saying to Brian Deal-a-Day Lane, 'I really don't feel well.' He offered to get someone to look at me but I just wanted to go home. 'I think it's just been a hard few months,' I suggested.

I remember getting back in the Mustang and driving home very slowly even though it was a very fast car, because – like at the gig – I had to think about everything very deliberately. It was like, *I need to turn left, I am going to put the indicator on, now I need to turn the wheel left* . . .

I got home and my missus Roz, who hadn't been at the show, asked how it had gone and I just said, 'Fine, but I really need to go to bed.' She said I'd probably been drinking too much but I hadn't, I just felt terrible. I thought a long night's sleep would see me right. I went to bed and fell fast asleep.

I woke up the next morning . . . and felt exactly the same.

I had an interview to do with Chris Hayes from *Melody Maker*; they used to do a piece made up of questions sent in from the public. *Melody Maker* would phone the person concerned and you'd give the answer over the phone, in person. Normally, I really enjoyed this feature, but I was still feeling like shit and when Chris phoned I didn't really respond very well.

'Are you all right, Rick?' he asked.

'No, I don't feel great. Can we do this another time? I'm so sorry.'

I put the phone down and went up the stairs . . . on my hands and knees. My arms felt like lead weights and I tried to get up but I couldn't. I shouted for Roz and when she came up I said, 'I think you'd better call a doctor . . . and an ambulance.'

The doctor arrived and came up to my room where he examined me and asked some poignant questions and then said, 'I'm going to give you an injection.' Within a couple of minutes, I started to feel quite good. I presumed it was a B_{12} injection, a massive rush of vitamins to kick-start my system and get me back on track.

'You will need to go to hospital for more checks, Mr Wakeman, I'm afraid.'

'But I feel much better since you gave me that injection.'

'You should do – I've pumped you full of morphine. In a few moments you won't be able to feel any pain whatsoever.'

He wouldn't even let me walk to the ambulance, I was

stretchered out of my own home. As they carted me across the driveway, my band arrived for a scheduled meeting.

'Rick, what's up?' said my singer, Ashley, looking very disturbed.

'Nothing really, Ash, I'll be back later so we can have the meeting then, OK.'

'OK, we'll see you in the Packhorse later, Rick.'

There are certain experiences in your life you won't forget and being wheeled on a trolley through a hospital is one of them. If you're going in for a leg plaster or maybe an X-ray, it's perhaps no big deal. But as I was wheeled past the various departments in Wexham Park Hospital, signs whizzed past me, and I tried to read them and second-guess where we were heading.

Then we stopped outside a large double door with a sign directly above it.

They pushed the doors open and started guiding my trolley through.

That's when I read the words above me.

It said 'Cardiac Arrest Unit'.

I was twenty-five.

I found myself in a quite big room and noticed that I had started shaking. I just kept thinking, *This can't be possible, I can't have had a heart attack*. Then this really nice doctor came and talked to me, she was called Dr Speed. She explained they would need to run extensive checks and then she said, 'I think you live life quite hard, Mr Wakeman – am I right?'

'You are.'

'Do you drink?'

'Oh, yes. Like a fish.'

'And smoke?'

'Only cigarettes. Like a chimney.'

'I see you are a rock musician. Do you take drugs?'

'Nope. Nothing.'

'It will show up if you are not telling the truth.'

Sitting in the chair used by David Hemmings in *Journey to the Centre of the Earth* at the Festival Hall in 1974.

My mum with five of my kids, taken back in the early 90s. From left to right, Oliver, Jemma, my mum, Ben, Oscar and Adam.

A very rare photograph of my gran with her great-grandchildren. From left to right, Adam, Jemma, Ben, my gran and Oliver.

I knew this bloody jacket was going to be itchy but I still bought it!

Another rare photo, this time taken at a performance of 1984. I am playing one of the first hand-held keyboards ever produced. Behind me are Tim Stone and Steve 'Boghead' Barnacle.

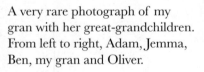

The Strawbs in 1970. From left to right, John Ford, Richard 'Hud' Hudson, Dave Cousins, me and Tony Hooper.

(*Left*) Aged twenty-six, at my little farm in Devon.

(*Below*) The classic line-up of the English rock ensemble from the mid-70s. From left to right, Ashley 'Fat Man of Pop' Holt, me, Martin Shields, Roger 'Budgie' Newell, Tony 'Greasy Wop' Fernandez, John 'Dusty' Dunstable, Reg Brooks, John 'Hodgy' Hodgson.

A long way from Perivale –
me in Switzerland in 1978.

Yes, in the late-70s.

Three newspaper cuttings.
They speak for themselves I think!

NEW MUSICAL EXPRESS

January 26, 1974   U.S. 50c/Canada 55c   9p

BOOK OF ROCK
Dylan 'Planet Waves' review

RONSON GOES SOLO

Rainbow concerts
PAGE 3

RICK WAKEMAN:
THE MAN,
HIS MUSIC,
HIS ULCER...
PAGE 22

1974
Readers'
Poll

TAX FAX

The GOOD guys

The BAD guys

POP EXTRA by Trevor Reynolds. Featuring a superstar, a top guitarist and B

The Biggs Sound—by Ric

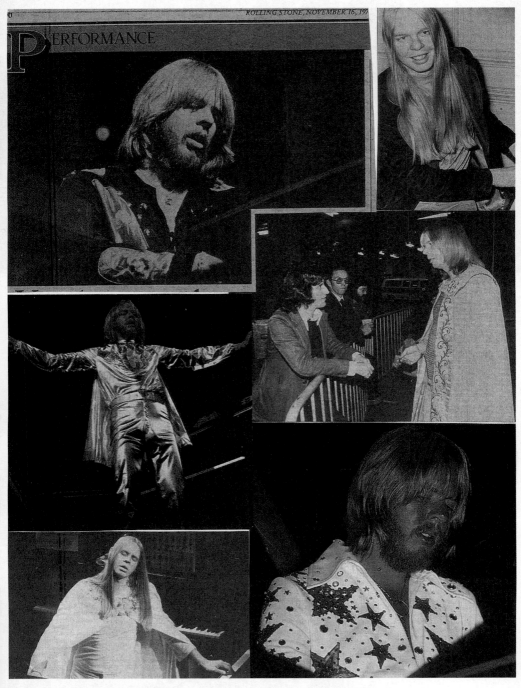

PERFORMANCE

Six shots of me throughout the 70s and 80s.
I'd probably be shot for real if I dressed up like that today!

This is the only photograph that I know of, of the band displaying their feelings at Wembley during the *King Arthur on Ice* concerts.

Me as the god Thor in the Ken Russell film *Listzomania*.

The poster of the film *Listzomania* … wish I had one.

ICE COOL RICK!

Mick Brown reports on Rick Wakeman's concert on ice at the Empire Pool Wembley

'Are you definitely saying you are going to have horses on ice, Rick?'

An amazing photograph of many of the cast of *King Arthur on Ice* at Wembley.

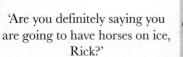

(*Overleaf*) Me in the *No Earthly Connection* cape in the late-70s.

IN CAMELOT, nature calls. "These bloody costumes are so authentic they don't even put flies in them", grimaces a knight, patting his chain mail in frustration. "They'd just piss themselves in the Middle Ages. That's why they smelt so awful . . ."

His friend stubs out a cigarette, pulls on his helmet and attempts to struggle into his

shoulders. "Fall over in this, love, and there's no way you'll be able to get up again. That's what I'm dreading . . ."

On stage Rick Wakeman is picking his nose for the benefit of a French television crew. The stage is a large, cumbersome tub afloat a sea of ice, its cardboard-battlement sides bursting at the seams with musicians and singers. Wakeman's keyboards are ranged on a raised dais centre-stage, 14 in number, some £20,000 worth of the most sophisticated wires, patches and circuitry available. Speakers, slungfrom gantries above the stage, give off a predatory buzz.

"We can't hear the choir",

turn off the buzz please. Can you just . . . please . . . bloody hell, TURN IT OFF. Thank you. And these lights. It's the Empire Pool, not the Empire Stadium. A concert, not a bloody football match." The lights blink out.

Wakeman turns to his keyboards. David Measham, conductor of the New World Symphony Orchestra, raises his baton. The two vocalists from Wakeman's English Rock Ensemble step to their microphones. The English Chamber Choir and the Nottingham Festival Group shuffle expectantly in their seats. The music swells into force, rumbling up into the rafters, rippling around the

knights step onto the ice and trace elegant circles around the stage. One scoots the breadth of the arena, executing a series of subtle twists and turns which culminate in an ignominious prat-fall. Oh, bloody hell . . .

"It's very dodgy", Rick allows, "because one man's meat is another man's poison. There are people who just want to go along to see a band, hear their songs, clap their hands and go home. I can understand that. And that's all some performers like to give their audience. There's others who try to bring, for want of a better word, *entertainment* into it; the theatrical side of things but without

'Drugs won't show up, I can guarantee it.'

'When you say you drink quite a lot, what do you mean exactly?'

I saw no point in not being honest.

'Very heavily – into double figures of pints of beer a day, plus probably a couple of bottles of wine and at least a bottle of Scotch.'

'Right, yes, we would consider that to be heavy drinking. Suicidal, actually. Well, I'm sorry to say you are exhibiting all the symptoms of having suffered a heart attack, Mr Wakeman. However, at your age, I'd like to investigate further because there might be other causes . . .'

One of these other possibilities that she explained was pericarditis, which I think in layman's terms means the heart has effectively caught a cold. That sounded far more preferable, so my spirits lifted considerably. They ran some ECGs and various other fairly invasive tests, then left me alone for two hours.

Your heart's just caught a cold, Rick, you'll be fine . . . I tried to reassure myself. Then Dr Speed returned, looking pretty grim. I knew it was bad news.

'Mr Wakeman, I'm afraid you have had a heart attack after all. In fact, we think you've had two. Not massive ones but you will have to stay here for between six and nine weeks. We have to get to the bottom of this.'

I was stunned.

It's amazing to think that nowadays you can have a quadruple bypass and be out within two days, wandering around and playing golf. Back then it was different: they thought it was best to keep as still as possible whereas now they know exercise is an essential part of the recovery.

They carted me off to the ward, where two more incredible – and very touching – things happened. First off, Jon Anderson came to see me. Although there had been no lasting acrimony when I left Yes, his was not a face I expected to see. Initially, it

57

was not the friendliest of splits because the other guys thought I should have hung on in there and tried to sort something out musically – maybe they were right, maybe I should have stayed and fought my corner . . . ?

Anyway, Jon came in and sat by my bed. He always used to call me Wake-Up.

'How are you, Wake-Up?' he said.

'I've been better, Jon, I have to admit. This isn't very nice.'

'Do you want to come back to the band?' he asked directly.

'No, Jon – why do you ask?'

'Because I need to satisfy my own mind that the reason you are here has nothing to do with your decision to leave the band.'

'Jon, that decision didn't have any bearing on my situation now. My lifestyle hasn't helped matters but it is certainly not the band decision that caused this. I still feel I made the right decision, by the way.'

'I needed to hear that from you,' said Jon, visibly relieved.

'Thank you very much and bless you for coming.'

I asked him if it had been a band decision to send him down, but he said no, it was purely a personal thing. I hate to use the word, but that little incident 'bonded' us; Jon and I had never really talked together very much in the previous three years I'd been in the band, but that time he came into the hospital set a marker for a friendship that has stayed there since.

I started to get bored in hospital, as you do, but then I discovered the fun I could have with the bromide tablets that were dished out daily. I collected as many as I could and when the consultants came round, always with their cup of tea, I used to slip a tablet in their drink. It's rumoured that bromide suppresses the sex drive, so I think during the six weeks I was in hospital, I influenced most of the consultants' sex lives. They certainly seemed to smile less as the weeks went by.

One day, my manager, Brian 'Deal-a-Day' Lane, came in with Dr Towers – a very esteemed man who actually did the first baboon-heart transplant on a human. He said to Deal-a-Day, 'Is Mr Wakeman financially secure?'

Why on earth does he need to know that? I thought.

'You see,' he continued, 'it looks as if Mr Wakeman really does need to take it easy from now on. It is obvious that his occupation is not entirely conducive to either an easy life or one bereft of temptation. I really have to advise him . . .' and at this point he looked straight at me, '. . . to stop the touring and the anti-social hours and excess, I really can't condone that in light of his current condition.'

I sat there listening and thinking, *Bugger that, I'm not going down that route, what else would I do?*

After the surgeon had left, it did nonetheless get me thinking about my finances and my future. If what he was saying was true and I could never tour again, then I needed some form of backup.

If that's the case, I better write another album, quick.

So that's how I came to write *King Arthur*.

I'd already started work to a small degree on the new project, but Crystal Palace and my failing health had snubbed out too much progress. So, picking up where I'd left off, I got some paper and pens and I wrote most of *King Arthur* in the hospital. Not surprisingly, perhaps, much of that project became quite auto-biographical – for example, because of my situation in the hospital, The Last Battle (the one where my skater friend had to commit suicide! You'll see . . .) was as much about my predicament as it was King Arthur's – there were a lot of parallels going on. I'll tell you more shortly.

Anyway, six weeks later I was discharged from hospital some way on the road to recovery. With Dr Towers's advice about not touring and not working long antisocial hours still ringing in my ears . . . I headed for the studio to record *King Arthur*.

So did I take any of his advice?

Not really, no.

I stopped smoking cigarettes as they insisted . . . but simply moved on to cigars; I did cut back on the drinking at first, but that didn't last long and within months I was downing vast amounts again.

Why?

I'm one of those people who does everything to excess. At that stage, I could not have gone out and had a glass or two of wine with dinner, it would have to be a couple of bottles and half a bottle of brandy.

When I smoked cigarettes, it was always thirty-plus a day.

I never had one car, I mean, at one point I had twenty-two.

Wives – I've had three divorces, and my fourth marriage is imminent.

Hair – long, down the back ideally.

I didn't just support a football club, I bought one.

Everything to excess: drink, cigarettes, cars, wives, hair, football . . . And they all cost me!

THE JOURNEY OF
THE HUMPING DINOSAURS

OK, I've kept you waiting, so now do you want to hear about those dinosaurs? Yes? You know all about *Journey to the Centre of the Earth* being a hit album, you've heard about me leaving Yes and having those heart attacks. What you don't know is the really important bit – the humping dinosaurs . . .

. . . Can I just tell you about Peter Sellers and my nan, first?

Then I'll do the humping dinosaurs, I promise.

It's an odd universe where Peter Sellers, one of the finest actors and comic geniuses in history, crosses paths with my nan; however, by explaining how these two titans came to meet, I will at least also explain how I came to be recording a musical version of Jules Vernes's classic novel *Journey to the Centre of the Earth*. We need to get in a time machine (sorry) and go back to before Crystal Palace, before I left Yes, and back to just after my slurred interview with Whispering Bob Harris on *The Old Grey Whistle Test*.

'Have you ever heard of the book *Journey to the Centre of the Earth*, Brian?' I asked Deal-a-Day Lane as I sat in his office.

'Of course I have, Rick,' came his blunt reply.

'Have you actually read it?'

It's one of those books that tons of people know about and even know the story fairly well, but haven't actually read. I've read it several times and I absolutely love it. Jules Vernes was a genius, a true visionary. His books dealt with science and science fiction generations before these ideas were in general circulation; he was actually a geologist and every book he wrote had huge elements of futuristic truth in them. He even got certain calculations such as the re-entry angle into the earth's atmosphere correct – he had a very specific expertise. We're talking about 1864 here. Genius. Ironically, a journey to the centre of the earth is one of the few predictions he made that has not come true although many of the geological facts he wrote are incredibly accurate.

So I said to Deal-a-Day, 'I want to do *Journey to the Centre of the Earth*.'

'What do you mean, Rick, dare I ask?'

'I want to do a full stage production, big orchestra, the works.'

'So it's not gonna be cheap then, Rick. One question, Rick . . .'

'Anything . . .'

'Why?'

I explained that it personally fascinated me and that also, from a commercial point of view, if you had a book that so many people thought they were familiar with – whether that was because of the film or the novel – then there was clearly a market for a production. Andrew Lloyd Webber and Tim Rice had this off to a tee by using stories that people at least knew a modicum about, or thought they did. The familiarity gives that comfort zone. It still made no sense to Deal-a-Day but I'd made my mind up. I consciously took a leaf out of David Bowie's book – he was a friend and had once said to me, 'If you want to move forward, you have to do what your musical heart wants you to do, otherwise all you are doing is what people would like to be able to do. But they won't have your imagination. Just go ahead.'

I knew the exact venue I wanted and I wasn't aiming low – the Royal Festival Hall. I spoke to David Measham who was one of the main conductors of the London Symphony Orchestra, as I'd played on the live show of *Tommy* with them with David conducting, and he said they were well up for it. I also contracted the English Chamber Choir so we were already talking about the very highest calibre of musicianship. Lou Reisner had produced the *Tommy* shows and I asked him to produce *Journey* for me, so the team was almost complete. Now all I needed was a band.

Deal-a-Day had a dream line-up sorted in his mind: I was old friends with John Entwistle of The Who from back in the day playing at the Red Lion pub, if you recall, and Brian said we could easily get Clapton in too. Aiming high, then!

'You are missing the point, though, Brian. This is not *my* album – when people come to the concert, I want them to be coming to see *Journey*, not coming to a show by Rick Wakeman and his celebrity musician friends.'

I had a much better idea.

Cue local boozer the Valiant Trooper.

On a Sunday night, I used to go down the Valiant Trooper to play with a great bunch of musicians, share a tale or two and a pint or ten. Yes were hot to trot at the time and I'd already had success with *The Six Wives of Henry VIII*, so I was used to playing with very high-profile and talented people. However, at the same time, I really, *thoroughly* enjoyed playing in such a relaxed atmosphere with the pub band from the Valiant Trooper. OK, it wasn't exactly Clapton and Entwistle.

We had Ashley Holt singing. I knew him from days spent playing at the Top Rank Ballroom in Watford.

We had Roger Newell on bass . . .

And Barney James on drums . . .

I added a session-guitarist friend of mine called Mike Egan, and the line-up was complete.

I tell you what, though, those boys could play. The pub wasn't that big and we used to have people cramming in there, regularly spilling out onto the car park. So one Sunday, after we'd played and were sinking a few afterwards, I enquired as to the band's availability.

'So, chaps. You got any gigs coming up over Christmas?'

'Oh, yeah, Rick, we've got some good bookings. There's the Nag's Head on the fourteenth of December and then we've got two gigs in two weeks at the White Hart.'

'Great, great. And have you got anything booked for mid-January?'

'Er, no, I don't think so, the Harrow's in the last week of January so we have got room. Why, what you got?'

'A couple of performances of something I've written called *Journey to the Centre of the Earth*,' I said as I was getting in my car.

'And where is it, Rick?'

'Er, the Royal Festival Hall.'

There was already a lot of press and public interest in *Journey*, so Brian Deal-a-Day was keen to hear my update.

'Did you get any joy out of Clapton and Entwistle, Rick?'

'Oh, I've got the band sorted, Brian.'

'Great. Who's in it?'

'Well, not Eric Clapton or John Entwistle. I've got Roger Newell, Ashley Holt . . .'

'Never heard of 'em, Rick.'

'Well, Ashley used to sing at the Top Rank Ballroom and I

play with all these guys every Sunday down at the Valiant Trooper.'

'Bloody marvellous. We have the premiere performance of this pioneering show, which we are recording live at the Royal Festival Hall with the London Symphony Orchestra and the English Chamber Choir, plus we are going to have the massed ranks of the world's music press, countless celebrities, dignitaries, politicians and pretty much every important person in the British music industry at this show and you've booked a bloody pub band.'

'That's about the size of it, Brian, yes.'

He called me a swear word.

With Brian's parting shot of 'It will all end in blood, never mind tears, Rick' ringing in my ears, I started rehearsals. They went great and I thoroughly enjoyed them. We secured the wonderful David Hemmings to be the narrator and, with the music all rehearsed and sorted, we were all set.

The only real glitch was with complimentary tickets. For some reason, the Royal Festival Hall hadn't held any back for me – for *anyone*, by all accounts. I had a lot of family, friends and business associates who I wanted to invite so I was most peeved. I tried everything I could to get some freebies but to absolutely no avail. The band and David Hemmings were also expecting their fair share of comps. Not even Deal-a-Day could get one and that really was saying something. So I had no alternative but to buy tickets from a tout.

For my own show.

I phoned up the late Stan Flashman, the legendary ticket tout and latter-day owner of Barnet FC, one of the all-time great larger-than-life characters. I remember the great goalkeeper Ray Clemence telling me about working with Stan at his football club and saying, 'It's always a bit strange when everyone gets paid out of a plastic bag.'

I rang Stan's number.

'Hello, Rick, what can I do for you? Bit early for Cup Final tickets, ain't ya?'

'Stan, you got any tickets for my show *Journey*? I can't get one anywhere.'

'Forty, Rick – how many do you want?'

'Forty, Stan.'

'Blimey, Rick, that's gonna cost ya.'

I bought forty tickets at three times the face value.

For my own show.

'I'm doing you a favour, Rick, I'm taking food off my own table here . . . but I tell you what I'll do . . . I'll throw in this year's Cup Final ticket for nothing.'

Stan Flashman, sadly missed.

Come the night of the two back-to-back performances at the Royal Festival Hall, and Deal-a-Day was anxious. Quite rightly, he pointed out that for all my laid-back approach to the band, this was a big deal for the Valiant Trooper's pub band and he suggested I make absolutely sure that they weren't crippled with nerves backstage. It seemed an astute observation and I agreed to find them out, weaving my way through the labyrinthine passages to their dressing room. With some trepidation, I knocked on the door and went in . . .

. . . They were playing darts.

They'd brought their own dartboard and seemed to have some sort of round robin competition going on.

'All right, guys, we're on in an hour.'

Barely looking up from their pints and arrows, they said, 'All right, Rick, great.'

Just as we were about to go on, David Hemmings came in and said to me, 'Peter Sellers is here, but apparently he's got someone else sitting between him and his missus, the Australian model Miranda Quarry.'

I reassured David that this was no problem, as clearly whoever was sitting alone in between one of the most famous movie stars on the planet and his glamorous partner would happily oblige and just switch seats.

Once I walked onstage, I was keen to survey the front rows to see who was there and spotted Ringo Starr straight away. Sure enough, there was Peter Sellers and, just as David Hemmings had said, two down from him was Miranda Quarry.

And who was sitting in between them . . . ?

My nan.

Bless her, she was well into her eighties and was sitting there in her smart hat and overcoat, while Peter Sellers and Miranda Quarry looked distinctly ruffled. Only years later did I find out what had actually happened.

Apparently, Peter introduced himself to my nan, who had absolutely no idea who he was. Then, very politely, he enquired if it would be possible to switch seats so that he might enjoy the performance sitting next to his wife.

She said, 'Where did you get your tickets from, young man?'

'Er, from the narrator of this evening's performance, a gentleman by the name of David Hemmings.'

'Do you know who gave me my ticket, F24?' my nan asked, showing him the stub.

'No,' said Peter Sellers.

'Rick gave it to me himself. He's my grandson, you know.'

'You must be very proud,' said Sellers. 'Now, would it be possible to switch seats please?'

'I thought I'd explained,' said my nan. 'Rick gave me F24, so that's where I'm sitting!'

And that's where she sat.

Right, it's time to tell you about the humping dinosaurs. Finally.

The Crystal Palace venue was chosen very carefully to suit the grandiose nature of the live show for *Journey*. This was not

67

a gig you could easily perform at the Timber Carriage. Although the venue was superb in many ways, it did come with a few difficulties. For a start, the area around Crystal Palace itself was littered with transmitters that the BBC used for radio and television. We are talking about fairly primitive early days for electronic equipment onstage, so there were often little glitches that only presented themselves at the most inappropriate moment. In the case of my show at Crystal Palace in front of 20,000 people, the particular technical gremlin that reared its head was the fact that my keyboards could pick up RF, or so-called Radio Frequency. In layman's terms, this meant that when you pressed the volume pedals, the keyboard picked up radio signals which were then channelled through the various link-ups and out through the stage PA.

In other words, my keyboards became the world's biggest radio receiver. The only way to get rid of these rogue signals was to play the keyboards. Then, and only then, would the radio (or for that matter sometimes the TV and occasionally a taxi rank) cease to be heard over the volume of the keyboards. So the most important thing was to keep the pedals flat down when playing and up when not.

The show was about to begin and, out of force of habit, I pushed one of the pedals down and suddenly, blasting out of the PA, came the classified football results. It was 27 July and, although the season hadn't started properly, all the friendlies were being played and how your team was shaping up for the new season was in every football fan's mind. Remember, this was decades before Teletext or footy results being texted to your mobile phone; the radio and television 'Final Scores' programmes were the only way that people could learn the day's results. Most papers printed the day's fixtures with blank lines on one page so that people could write the scores down as they were read out.

So I stood on that enormous stage and, at 120 decibels, all 20,000 of us heard, 'Arsenal 2, Bolton 0 . . . Leicester City 2, Aston Villa 2 . . .' Now, you might think this was a disaster but virtually everyone in the crowd just pulled their *Evening News* out of their pockets and started writing the scores down. The only gasps came when it transpired that Everton had beaten Manchester United or some such unexpected drama. Myself and the band just waited five minutes until they'd read out all the scores and then carried on as if nothing untoward had happened.

Although the technology might not sound too sophisticated (it was for the day), I had a field day with stage props for *Journey*. In case you haven't been to Crystal Palace, there's a fairly sizeable lake in front of the stage. Bearing in mind the content of *Journey*, it seemed an ideal chance to indulge myself.

So I had this bloody great pair of inflatable dinosaurs specially made in Holland. One was an ichthyosaurus. The other was a plesiosaur. In their day, they both tipped the scales at several tons and towered well above the 30-foot mark. No point in doing things by halves, I always say.

I wish I didn't always say that, because these dinosaurs cost me a bloody fortune.

Still, they looked brilliant: bear in mind this was the mid-1970s and stage props like this were relatively unknown and risky. By definition, as this was the first time inflatable dinosaurs had been hand-built for a rock gig, we found out the practical difficulties as we went along. For a start, the air pressure inside these beasts had to be kept at a constant level, otherwise they very quickly began to deflate, collapse and lose all their shape. It took absolutely ages to fully reinflate them, so maintaining the air pressure was crucial.

We placed the dinosaurs beneath the surface of the lake at the front of the stage and when we started to play the song 'The

Battle' they inflated, emerging from out of the water, and by carefully controlling the air pumps we could make them move a little and appear to be having a sort of fight.

I was playing my keyboards and watching all this – it looked *fantastic*. It had all gone perfectly to plan until one of the dinosaurs got snagged on something and, unfortunately, sprung a leak.

It wasn't a big leak, but it was a leak nonetheless. And it was right at the base of its tail, a veritable orifice, so it was very difficult for the crew to carry out any kind of swift emergency repair. This wasn't the biggest problem, however. The worst part was that the hole from the snag was very small, but the air pressure inside this ginormous dinosaur balloon was extremely high, so basically this creature farted its way through the entire performance at a quite serious volume. As you know, I was about to suffer two heart attacks so I had other things on my mind, and besides, no one at the show seemed to really notice.

Just like the Chinese lantern tunnels we created for Yes, when we came to take the *Journey* show to America the crew pleaded with me not to use these inflatable farting dinosaurs. They pointed out the fragility and the difficulty of setting them up, the possibility of them getting destroyed in transit, and also made the perfectly valid point that a fart lost in the ether of an open-air show at Crystal Palace would most likely sound like a nuclear explosion in a smaller enclosed arena gig in the States.

I was having none of it.

We flight-cased the dinosaurs ready for America.

Sure enough, there were a few small tears when we got to America but, undeterred, I said, 'What you need is a giant bicycle-repair kit, chaps.' As predicted by the crew, however, the dinosaurs repeatedly ended up with loads of punctures and by halfway through the US dates – and after God knows how many giant bicycle repairs – you could tell that the roadies had had enough. Every night they would lug in the conventional gear and stage set, then you could see they were all avoiding being lumbered with the dinosaur duty. Cue more grumbling all round.

This routine repeated itself throughout the tour until one night at a show in the Deep South, right in the Bible Belt. I walked into the soundcheck and enquired after the health of the dinosaurs, fully expecting the usual chorus of complaints and moans.

'Absolutely fine, Rick, no probs,' came the surprising reply.

I should have known at that moment that something was going on.

'You sure? No tears, no grumbles, nothing to worry about?'

'Nothing, Rick. The stage is a little cramped on one side so both dinosaurs will be on stage left, but apart from that, all sorted.' That had happened before so I thought nothing of it.

Fast-forward to halfway through the concert and it was all going swimmingly. The dinosaurs were working perfectly and the crowd were loving every minute of the dramatic performance.

Unfortunately, it was about to get a whole lot more dramatic.

Unbeknown to me, the crew had discovered that by carefully reducing the air pressure in the dinosaurs and then suddenly reinflating them at a rapid rate, they could make it look like the dinosaurs were shagging each other. That's why you pay good money to get the best technical brains that the music business has to offer.

At first I didn't notice. I could see the ichthyosaurus was leaning towards the plesiosaur but thought nothing of it and carried on playing. I was right in the middle of a particularly difficult and demanding piece of music when I looked up from my keyboards to see both dinosaurs rampantly humping each other at the

71

front of the stage, up and down, up and down, while the bemused audience sat in shocked near-silence. The beasts' humping got faster and faster and more animated until, just before the end of the battle sequence, the plesiosaur let out the most enormous fart and then deflated.

The reviews in the Bible-Bashing Belt media the next day were not the best I've ever had, let's just put it like that.

THE HEALTHIEST
MAN ON EARTH

I told you I'd come back to *The Myths and Legends of King Arthur and the Knights of the Round Table*, so here goes.

No one can criticise me for keeping things simple.

Well, that's not true actually – my management did.

By the 1970s I'd moved on from Mervyn Conn Artists and was now, as a member of Yes, 'looked after' by another legend in the business – Brian 'Deal-a-Day' Lane.

Before I go all medieval on you, let me tell you a small anecdote about Deal-a-Day.

Deal-a-Day was actually the epitome of the great rock 'n' roll manager. On the very first tour I did with Yes, we arrived at a quite swanky hotel in America, checked in, unpacked and then met back at reception. It was a courtyard hotel where the chalet rooms were all the way around the perimeter and in the middle there was a beautiful swimming pool. Our bassist Chris Squire wanted to catch some sleep – he was well known then, and still is, for going to sleep. He sleeps non-stop, you can't get him up until one or two in the afternoon, he just sleeps and sleeps. By contrast, if the sun was even remotely out in the sky, our singer

Jon Anderson would be out sunbathing. So he led the way out to the pool. We were all congregating at reception and I said, 'What's everyone going to do before sound check, then?'

Chris replied, 'I'm going to go to my room and lie on the bed.'

'I'm going to lie by the pool,' said Jon.

Then Deal-a-Day piped up: '. . . And I'm going to go and lie on the phone.'

Right, introduction over, back to the Middle Ages.

Well, 1975.

Picture the scene. I'm in a meeting with Harvey Goldsmith, the most famous promoter and agent in the history of rock 'n' roll, and Deal-a-Day Lane in his Notting Hill Gate office. We are discussing the dozens of ideas I've had about how to perform *King Arthur* live.

'OK, so I'm thinking a castle, horses, knights, Middle Ages costumes, at Wembley Empire Pool . . .'

'It's going to cost a fortune, Rick,' winced Deal-a-Day. 'We should at least do it at the Royal Albert Hall.'

'I don't want to do it at the Albert Hall, the acoustics are rubbish and, besides, I can't build a castle in the Royal Albert Hall. I want to do it at Wembley.'

'You can't do it at Wembley, Rick,' said Harvey.

'Why not?'

I can vividly remember Brian's smug face as Harvey replied, 'Because the dates you want are right before *Holiday on Ice* and it takes three weeks for them to install and then freeze the ice rink, so there's just no way we can do it.'

I was not to be deterred.

'Well, I'll do it on ice, then . . .'

'Rick, don't be bloody ridiculous, it ain't gonna happen . . . now go and think about the Royal Albert Hall.'

I did think about it . . . and dismissed it. I came out of the office, jumped in my car and drove straight to Fleet Street, parked by Farringdon Road, walked round to Red Lion Square and into the Red Lion pub. Chris Welch, the editor of *Melody Maker*, was there.

As we lifted the first pint, I said, 'Chris, I've got an exclusive for you. I'm doing *King Arthur*, full symphony orchestra, English Chamber Choir, a male-voice choir . . .'

'Blimey, Rick, that's pretty ambitious . . .'

'. . . And a full band . . .'

'Crikey . . .'

'. . . In a castle . . .'

'Right . . . anything else?

'. . . On ice.'

I was making it up as I went along, to be brutally honest, sitting there telling Chris about all these grand designs for a full medieval pageant, horses, knights, the lot – it all sounded brilliant, not least because it was the first time I'd heard it too. He asked how we'd set up the PA if I was in the middle and I said I would ship in a Clair Brothers PA from America, as they would be skilled in rigging for such a concert and nobody in the UK was capable of doing it at that time. The PA would be hung and suspended in the middle, in netting, for surround sound.

'Rick, this is front page! Can I run it?'

'You're welcome to it – help yourself.'

Two days later, when *Melody Maker* hit the news-stands, Deal-a-Day Lane phoned me up and referred to me using a very brief and specific gynaecological word. Once I'd denied being that, he said, 'What the hell have you done, Rick?'

'Well, it's more about what I'm going to do, Brian . . . *King Arthur* on ice.'

I was really pleased with myself. But then I went to a meeting at the management office and they told me what it was going to cost.

It was not going to be cheap.

In fact, it was disastrous and even with sell-out performances it was going to cost me a lot more money to put the show on than it was ever going to make. Remember, this was before the days of sponsorship, before TV bought pay-per-view concert rights in advance, before videos and DVDs of shows helped subsidise tours. It would all have to be funded through ticket sales. Deal-a-Day sat me down with the accountant, David Moss, a lovely man who said, 'Rick, if you sell out three nights at Wembley Empire Pool you will lose this amount of money.' And he pointed at what appeared to be someone's phone number on a scrap of paper.

'It's not too late to call it off,' Brian said hopefully.

'No, no, no! We can't call it off. By the way, I think it's going to cost more than that. We haven't budgeted correctly for the ice skaters.'

Believe it or not, I actually knew a little bit about ice skating and was therefore aware that most top skaters lived in Eastern Europe and Australia so we'd have to fly them in and put them up somewhere for the duration of the shows. So we did the figures again and all agreed on the amount I was set to lose. It was similar to the national debt of Paraguay.

You will recall how worried I was when I realised there was still a KGB uniform in my suitcase as I sat in Igor's security office in Russia. Looking at the colossal loss I stood to make on *King Arthur on Ice* was the exact opposite feeling. I was reading about 9.8 on the 'Don't-Give-a-Toss-o-Meter' by this point.

'If it's going to be done, it should be done properly. Decision made, chaps. *King Arthur on Ice* it is!'

Building the set was like being involved in one of the Seven Wonders of the Modern World. We started to get the castle built first and I spent hours and hours in meetings with carpenters and builders, explaining about ramparts and how they would need to accommodate the orchestra and the choirs. At the same time, we'd shipped in the skaters and were rehearsing them like crazy. I was loving every minute.

Meanwhile, the media were all over the idea. They were particularly interested in my having said there'd be horses involved.

On ice.

'Are you definitely saying you are going to have horses on ice, Rick?'

'Absolutely, it's going to be fantastic. There will be a lot of horses.'

By the time we got to three days before the three performances, all the tickets had sold out but the RSPCA, an organisation for the prevention of cruelty to animals and even Brent Council were mercilessly interrogating me about the possible dangers to these horses.

I calmly explained that we'd created these special stables outside Wembley, down by the artists' parking area, and that everything was in order. I then invited about fifty of the world's biggest newspapers and magazines down to show them these horses. The RSPCA and Brent Council representatives were there too, plus protesters ready to spit feathers when we unveiled the animals.

Except they weren't *actual* horses, were they?

I'd never said that.

I'd just said there'd be 'horses'. In this particular case, they were men on hobby horses. Skating round through dry ice so you could only see their top halves. To be fair, there wasn't one journalist who didn't laugh when these dozen or so blokes on pantomime steeds trotted out. Even the RSPCA people laughed, because they saw the funny side and were just glad it wasn't an issue. The only people who didn't laugh were the ones from Brent Council, who were just slightly left of Stalin. They didn't like it one bit.

Come the actual performances, I absolutely loved every second. There are two defining moments from the *King Arthur on Ice* shows that stick in my mind. Firstly, the nuns. The opening night had gone brilliantly. At the end of the first half, we had about a dozen female skaters dancing around in a Charleston style: it was really very striking, a great little taster for the second half. When they'd finished, I used to say to the band, 'Hey, guys, what do you think of that?' and they'd hold up score cards with 9s and 8s on them. Then I'd say, 'And what do you say to working for me for nothing?' At which point they'd flip the cards over to spell out the word 'Bollocks'. The audience loved it and it was all good fun.

On the second night, however, I hadn't really looked around the audience before I got to this section. I was just introducing the 'score cards sketch' when my eyes fell upon the seating block nearest to where the cards would be held aloft . . . it was full of nuns. There must have been 200 nuns sitting there, all pristine and proper.

Right on time, but with a sinking feeling in my stomach, I asked for the scores and the band duly held up some 9s and some 8s. The nuns all chuckled and a few polite handclaps rippled across the ice from their seats. I had no intention of making the joke about working for nothing but, unfortunately, the band didn't know that and just wanted to hit their cue.

Which they did, beautifully.

Bollocks.

The nuns howled with laughter!

The second defining moment of *King Arthur on Ice* was on the last night. Before the show, Tony Burdfield came to me and said, 'Rick, do you know you're one skater short? One of them is off sick.'

I wasn't too bothered. 'That's all right, Tony, there's that many of them . . .'

'Yes, but Rick . . .'

'Tony, no one will notice, don't worry.'

'OK, Rick, I'm just letting you know . . .'

The show was going along swimmingly until we came to a piece called 'The Last Battle'. It was a fantastic sight, I have to say, all these magnificent skaters dressed as knights with their wooden swords, an incredible light show, dry ice everywhere, it was remarkable. Out of the dry ice these horses' heads were visible, twenty-five on each side of the rink facing off for the final climactic battle. They would then skate around and face each other in pairs, where they would have a choreographed sword fight before simultaneously 'killing' each other and disappearing beneath the dry ice.

Just as 'The Last Battle' commenced, the penny dropped as to why Tony was worried about having a skater off sick. He was one of the knights which meant we had an odd number, twenty-four on one side and twenty-five on the other. The consequences were dawning on me too late, however; the knights were swirling around the rink majestically and then, bang on schedule, paired up to commence their sword fights and finish each other off.

Except of course for the one odd skater who was floating around aimlessly, looking for someone to kill and be killed himself. He was out of luck. His intended target – the missing knight – was at home in bed with gastroenteritis.

By now, the orchestra, the band, the choirs, the lighting crew, everyone had twigged. I remember David Measham, the conductor, looking at me and I just mouthed, 'Keep going, keep going!'

By now, the audience were starting to do the maths too so, as the numbers of knights dwindled, all eyes were on this lone warrior. The poor sod was skating around on his own, trying desperately to look like it was all planned. Eventually, of course, there was no one left but him and so for about a minute he skated around the rink, the whole of Wembley Empire Pool looking at him in anticipation. It felt like an eternity.

How he thought to do what he did next I will never know. But it was pure genius.

He simply stopped, plunged his sword into himself and committed suicide.

Genius.

It was a work of art.

King Arthur on Ice was one of the best times of my life. I loved every single minute: the preparation, the rehearsals, the music, the performances, everything. I would give my right arm to do it all again. It has gone down in rock 'n' roll folklore as one of the most extravagant shows of all time. In the countless polls that magazines like *Q* run every year, it nearly always comes out in the top three in both the 'Best Live Show' and the 'Biggest Folly' sections. I don't care about the latter, it was amazing. We were pioneering. This wasn't a 3-D hologram castle, we built the bloody thing out of wood. It wasn't special effects, it was all human-led, real life in front of your eyes. As far as I know, it was the first time a hung PA had been used in the UK. In many ways, those three nights on ice were very innovative. There is nothing to beat what I call a 'human spectacular' where everything that is going on is created by people – musicians, singers, actors, dancers and so on.

Everyone who took part in *King Arthur on Ice* has a story to tell.

A few years back, I spoke to the skating superstar Robin Cousins about the show and he was telling me that the technology has advanced so much that we could now do so much more: the ice doesn't need to be flat, they can freeze a rink much, much faster and you can even tour these shows. America would have been perfect because they have ice hockey stadiums absolutely everywhere; Eastern Europe likewise, albeit only once the Wall had come down. But back when I did it, the logistics meant it simply wasn't a show that could stand on its own two feet (or skates), even selling 15,000 tickets every night. So, sadly, we only ever did those three nights; I've performed *King Arthur* all over the world but only ever three times on ice.

Of course, as the money men had predicted, I lost a fortune across those three nights. But within eighteen months the *King Arthur* album had sold an extra 10 million copies.

Absolutely priceless.

When a musician tours, he or she needs insurance. It's not just for their own health cover, it also deals with what might happen if 10,000 people get to a show having paid for tickets and the show is cancelled for one reason or another. Insurers know the rock world isn't the safest of places to issue premiums, but there are several risk-takers who deal with this kind of business.

When it came to taking *King Arthur* to America (without the ice extravaganza), I could understand why insurers weren't beating a path to my door to cover me. I was only in my mid-twenties and had already had two heart attacks. I was under strict medical advice to stop smoking and drinking, both of which I patently wasn't doing. I was on tablets that were like little capsules of TNT and were designed to pretty much blow up your veins if you felt chest pains to allow any clot to pass through. And, finally, I was about to fly out to perform several highly demanding and lengthy shows across numerous American states, all the time inhabiting the far-from-healthy world of rock 'n' roll.

I was expecting a pretty horrid premium.

In fact, not one single insurer would touch me with a bargepole.

Not one.

The shows were already booked.

So I decided to go without insurance.

We made an agreement with the promoters that before each show I would have an ECG and if that said my ticker wasn't about to implode, then we'd do the gig. It was a long tour and it was quite some logistical achievement to get an ECG before every show but somehow we did it. I learned not to have one too soon after landing in a plane, as that can affect your heart rate hugely. Tricks of the trade, eh?!

I also learned that my heart rate and ECG reading seemed to improve vastly depending on how many free tickets to the show I handed the hospital staff. I was doing really good business at the time with two Top 5 albums, so tickets were pretty scarce. I'd go in for an ECG and they'd come in, start wiring me up and – you could almost time them – they'd say, 'Rick, you don't, by any chance, sorry to ask, have any tickets for tonight?'

'Yes, of course . . .' and then they'd do the ECG.

Which, if I failed, would mean the cancellation of the show that they'd just been given free backstage passes for.

Not the most objective of medical advice.

Night after night, according to the paperwork, I was one of the fittest, healthiest men on earth.

HERR SCHMIDT'S
FISHING TRIP

I tell you one thing that's a pain in the backside when you are a touring musician. Bloody visas. I've lost count of the number of times I've had visas go adrift or arrive late. The problem nearly sent me to a Siberian labour camp once, as you know, but that wasn't the last time I had troubles.

Take Paraguay in 1980. I was living in the south of France at the time – I didn't really want to live there but my missus did, so that was where I lived. I was booked on a tour of Brazil but there was a problem with my visa.

Oddly, there was a rule about the 'featured artist' which stated that only the main performer needed a visa, while his supporting band didn't. So my band could travel there without a hitch, but I was stranded. At the time I had a tour manager called Barry the Perv. Most of the band used to buy *Autotrader* to read on the various bus and plane journeys but Barry would always turn up with a copy of *Underwear Unlimited* or some other seedy little top-shelf mag. And he used to sweat quite profusely.

I tell you what, though: apart from being a sweaty perv, he was a great tour manager and a very funny guy.

So I get this phone call from Barry the Perv. He explained that Joan Baez had recently been in Brazil and at her opening press conference had laid on some fairly heavy political criticism of the government. The authorities did not take to this lightly and had subsequently stopped her from playing the shows.

'So why is this a problem for me, Barry?'

'Because they've stopped issuing visas to visiting featured artists until further notice, Rick.'

Great.

'But it's all right, Rick,' continued Barry the Perv, 'I've spoken to the promoter and the right backhanders are being dropped in all the right places. I can't get a visa before you go, but you can get to Rio posing as a tourist, and then we can go from there.'

Sounded like a plan.

I arrived in Rio and waltzed through passport control and customs. I was very well known in Brazil at the time and probably the only ones unaware that I was there for a tour were those in cemeteries.

'Are you just holidaying, sir?' etc., etc. 'Yes, yes . . .' and I was through. Barry had already arrived so we scooted off to the hotel to meet the promoter. When we got there, the promoter walked into the room and said, 'Right, welcome to Brazil, Mr Wakeman. Now you've got to go to Paraguay.'

'What? Right now? Why?'

'No, relax . . . in the morning. To get your work visa. They are not issuing them here, as you know, but we have arranged a back-dated one to be issued in Paraguay. You will be met at Asunción airport – here are your tickets, here is an envelope,' he explained. 'Hand this envelope to the man at the visa office in Asunción.'

'I'm not handing over any envelope,' I interjected, 'to anyone in Paraguay without knowing what's in it.'

'There's five $20 bills, Rick. Barry will go with you, he must travel too.'

So we were all set – all we had to do was travel under the false pretence of being tourists to a country with a collapsing economy and a legacy of SS- and Nazi-sympathising, where we would hand over an envelope to a complete stranger in exchange for what I was now beginning to realise was probably not the most 'legitimate' work visa.

Barry had started sweating (without the use of one of his many magazines).

When we landed at the airport in Paraguay I was surprised to be met by quite an entourage, including a television crew. I was not surprised to find that the man in charge was German. He was old and appeared to have a leg missing. Much later, I found out he was a former Second World War pilot. So off to a flying start, then – if you'll excuse the pun.

No 'Welcome to Paraguay' this time. The boss man just briskly shook our hands and said, 'Please come viz me.' The entourage – all with strong German accents – led us to a large blacked-out Mercedes, opened the doors and we climbed in. The car then glided out of the airport – no customs this time – and into the streets.

I was sitting there with Barry the Perv, taking this all in while looking out of the window at the passing scenery. There were hundreds of normal houses but then every few miles you'd see a huge mansion with a big driveway and the occasional swastika on the gate.

'I don't like this, Rick, I don't like this at all,' said Barry, sweating.

'Look, just keep calm, we're here now. If you want to get paid for the show, the show has to happen and for the show to happen we have to do this. It'll be all right.'

We arrived at a hotel and were given separate rooms. Another man with a German accent came into my room and said, 'You may phone for ze room service. There is not ze room service at zis hotel, but for you two, zey will bring ze food. You can go to ze bar but do not leave ze hotel.'

At that exact moment, Barry the Perv bounced into the room and shouted, 'Rick, I'm trying to phone England and I can't get a sodding outside telephone line . . .'

Ze German looked at Barry and then at me, one single precise eyebrow raised.

'You're not helping matters here, Barry,' I pointed out.

We were politely informed that we were not allowed to make any phone calls either.

'Ve vill pick you up in ze morning. I repeat, do not leave ze hotel.'

Once again I was waiting for Harry Palmer to walk into the room.

He didn't, nor did Michael Caine.

I had Barry the Perv.

We went to the bar and sank more than a few drinks. The Germans were actually very nice folk, likewise the people of Paraguay. (I have a theory that if you are in a band and a drinker, people are more accommodating; if you are known as a druggie band, people can be a lot less tolerant, as many of my peers found out.)

The next morning, the Germans arrived as agreed. We got back in the Merc and drove off to a town just outside Asunción. It seemed quite a small place, so I was sure that we'd soon see an embassy or official-looking building looming large around a corner.

Then the car started to slow down.

And stopped outside a newsagent.

'What are we doing here?' I asked, thinking that someone needed a paper.

'Up zeez stairs, zis is ze Brazilian embassy.'

Above a bloody sweet shop.

'You vill meet zis man, he is a Brazilian, he vill sort out ze visa.'

I dutifully climbed these rickety stairs to this tiny room above the sweet shop, a million miles from Mervyn Conn's solid oak staircase in the West End. At the end of the landing was a small room, just big enough for about four people to fit in, with a glass partition in the facing wall much like the ones you get at a doctor's reception. A woman opened the glass sliding panel, said, 'Yes, take a seat,' then went out of view and appeared from behind a door, beckoning me through. Inside this room there were six wooden chairs and little else.

We sat down and waited.

Barry was sweating. A *lot*. He was getting very paranoid.

'We are going to get killed, Rick,' he was saying. I noticed he wasn't browsing through a mag from his extensive porn collection now. 'We're never going to be seen again, Rick,' he continued.

'Barry, if you don't bloody well shut up, I'll make sure *you*'re never going to be seen again.'

 We were told to go back through the door where we would be dealt with by – and I am not making this up – a Herr Schmidt. The glass sliding panel opened again and the lady asked us exactly what we were there for.

'I am here to see Herr Schmidt about a visa.'

She said, 'Vait here,' and closed the partition. A minute later, she opened it again and said, 'He has gone fishing.'

This was nuts.

I explained that we had flown all the way from Brazil and had been brought here and that it would all be sorted. No one had mentioned 'ze fishing'.

She didn't move an inch.

Then I remembered the envelope in my pocket, so I pulled that out and said, 'Oh yes, I was asked to give this to you.' Without speaking, she turned and went back into the room. A minute or so passed and then she returned.

'Herr Schmidt has come back from ze fishing. Your passport please . . .'

Ten minutes later she returned and handed me my passport back, as well as a sealed envelope.

'Ze visa, goodbye.'

With Barry leading the way, we walked fairly briskly down the stairs, through the sweet shop, out into the street and got in the waiting Mercedes. I ripped open the envelope with my passport in it.

Now, a Brazilian government visa is actually quite snazzy, it's stamped very boldly and is actually quite splendid to look at.

Unlike what I was looking at in my passport.

The 'visa' I had been given appeared to be a wax crayon drawing by a five-year-old. The only thing missing was a picture of a house with smoke coming out of the chimney.

'Oh, shit!'

Anyway, we got back to the airport ready to use this crayon drawing to get me back into Brazil. But when we looked up at the departures board, there wasn't a single flight to Rio. I pointed this out to our one-legged German friend who was seeing us off, but he just said, 'You just go through, ze flight to Rio vill be there.'

Completely out of the blue, as we walked through the (non-existent) customs, One Leg said, 'I vould like you to come und play in our country one day.' Then he said, 'I hope you have found your trip here to be satisfactory.' Then he left, without another word. (I did actually return to play in Paraguay a few years later and loved it. The Paraguayan people are very special, as indeed are all South and Central American people that I've met. I just love visiting that part of the world.)

We went through to Departures and were met by a couple of men in official-looking uniforms who took us through a walkway and onto a Boeing 707 which, apparently, was flying to Rio after all. By the time we'd settled into our first-class seats Barry was sweating profusely again but we were both hugely relieved. There wasn't anyone else in first class but that wasn't unusual in South

America. The flight took off and after the seat-belt signs were turned off Barry the Perv went through the curtain to go to the gents. He came back only a few seconds later, as white as my friend Igor in Moscow had been.

'What's up, Barry?'

'Rick, there's no one else on this plane. We are the only two passengers . . .'

'Are you sure . . . ?' I got up and looked through the dividing curtains and, sure enough, we were the only two passengers on this massive Boeing.

'I don't like this, Rick, I don't like this at all,' said Barry, now making squelching noises every time he moved as he had sweated so much. 'We are going to get killed, Rick, we're never going to be seen again, Rick . . .'

'Oh, shut up, Barry, don't start that again, or else there'll only be one passenger on this bloody plane . . . it's probably the promoter, they've probably laid it on for us to get it all sorted . . .'

'What? A sodding 707?' pointed out Barry, justifiably.

Well, believe it or not, we flew straight to Rio and landed safely, without a hitch and with a fair few welcome drinks sunk. We disembarked and headed off to Arrivals. With my wax crayon visa drawing.

'Can't we just say we are on holiday, Rick?'

'Barry, not this close to the shows, it was in the papers yesterday with my photograph and we've sold 10,000 tickets, I can hardly say I've come for bird-spotting.'

When the customs officer opened up my passport to look at the work 'visa', I swear to God he just laughed out loud. So funny was it that he called over his two friends who in turn burst out giggling. They were literally pissing themselves laughing. By this point, Barry the Perv was just a human sweat bead. I thought he was going to explode and – I have to be honest – I also thought I was looking at a long stretch in a

Brazilian prison now, rather than a Siberian labour camp. Either way, I was stuffed.

Then, suddenly, with their laughs still subsiding, they stamped my passport and said, 'Go on through, have a great concert. Welcome to Brazil.'

THE VICTOR,
THE CONSUL AND THE ROLLER

I love cars. I've had a few in my time. As I mentioned, I had twenty-two at one time (although admittedly they were part of an exotic car-hire company that I owned called the Fragile Carriage Company) and I think I've been through about 200 altogether. It was a love affair that started when I was very young.

Let me take you back to my very first car, a beautiful Ford Anglia. I was only seventeen when I bought it and I thought I was the King of the Road. The car was a necessity because of all the equipment I had to cart around and my dad couldn't keep on acting as an unpaid roadie. So as soon as I passed my test, I decided to get a car.

Everyone I knew locally bought their first car from UC Slim Motors in Sudbury Town. It was the best car dealership on earth. It's long gone now, replaced by a shiny new operation that sells expensive Mercedes; back then it was a dump, but I loved going down there. I say dealership, it was more of a car lot. Well, street corner, really. With a dilapidated Portakabin.

It was run by a Mr Slim.

When you reached the ripe old age of seventeen, you would

head off to Sudbury Town to see Slim and tell him what you wanted, how much money you had, and he'd set you up . . . quite literally sometimes. Absolute death traps, every single one of them, but it didn't matter back then because there was no MOT law, nobody cared and, besides, the sort of cars us lads could afford barely did 30 m.p.h. flat out.

I'd saved up £30 and introduced myself to Mr Slim.

'First car is it, boy?' he said.

'Yes, Mr Slim.'

'How much you got?'

I told him and he said, 'Is that to include tax and insurance?' To which I replied 'Yes.'

'All right, son, I've got something in mind, follow me . . .'

He escorted me out of the office and straight over to an absolutely rust-ridden 1957 Ford Anglia. It had been blue, originally. I looked through the back windows and could see the concrete forecourt of the car lot – because the floor of the car was missing. None of the dials worked. I took it out for a test drive. The dashboard didn't light up at all so at night you would have no idea how fast you were going – although with the state of the engine you'd have a pretty good idea that it wasn't very fast. What I didn't know then was that it was also notoriously unreliable and would never start in the morning or if it had been left for more than six hours. Perhaps most notably, when you braked the car turned right. This might sound somewhat lethal, and it was, but I quickly learned how to drive it regardless. It was really no trouble – you just knew that if you needed to brake you also had to yank the steering wheel to the left at the same time to keep yourself in a straight line.

It was wonderful. I wanted it.

'I tell you what, son. This is a special car but just for you I'll do the motor and the insurance and I'll even get one of the lads to nip down to the post office and do your tax for you – yours for £30.'

I couldn't give Mr Slim the money quick enough.

About half an hour later, his 'mate' had come back from the post office with this tax disc and Slim handed me the keys and the insurance 'cover note' from a company called Cloverleaf. Years later, it transpired that him and his 'mate' actually just had a dodgy insurance pad and wrote out completely useless 'cover notes' as a way of getting us lads on the road. Looking back, I should have known this wasn't exactly comprehensive cover when Slim leaned over to me and whispered, 'Try not to claim.'

I had some great times in the Ford Anglia. I was still at school so driving your own car made me quite the big man. Even better was when I borrowed my dad's Standard Ensign. It had brakes, which was a huge improvement on the Ford Anglia. The Ensign had three working gears and a dashboard that lit up. I could get all my gear in it so when I had an important show I'd ask my dad if I could borrow his car.

One year, the Ensign was to play an unwitting role in one of my more renowned and memorable gigs. I'd met a Salvation Army trumpet player during a residency with the Atlantic Blues in Neasden – a brilliant West Indian kid who, like me, was a huge fan of Otis Redding and Wilson Pickett, all the soul stuff. 'I know all their tunes, I sing them all day in my bedroom and I know all the brass riffs,' he told me. At the time, dance nights usually went one of two ways – either down the Gerry and the Pacemakers route or down this American path towards Otis and friends. I found myself far more attracted to this soul material and was keen to play some of it live. We exchanged numbers and said how great it would be to play together some time.

Now, each year the school held a dance where a live band played. The deputy head teacher, Mr Wright, had somehow heard through the grapevine that I was in a band (and I must admit I had mentioned to a few friends in the school playground that I had this black American soul singer in my band) and

I was somewhat taken aback when he asked me if I would bring my band for the night. And mistakenly he said, 'I hear you might have a black American soul singer in your band, Wakeman?'

Even more mistakenly, I said, 'Yes.'

I vividly remember standing there thinking to myself, *How are you going to get out of this one?*

Truth was, though, that I just wanted to *play* (and here was an opportunity to work with this guy I'd met from the Salvation Army band) so a tiny little white lie about nationality was splitting hairs. I shat myself for about three days until I came across his number. I phoned him there and then.

'Hey, do you want to sing "Mustang Sally", "Shake" and "Midnight Hour" and other numbers like that? With my band, at a school dance?'

'Oh, yeah!' He was so excited.

We rehearsed with other musician friends soon after and he was brilliant, absolutely sensational. I was really excited myself until I told him the time of the school dance. The problem was, he couldn't get there very early as he worked for London Transport as a bus conductor and had to finish his shift first, then get home, change out of his work clothes, put his stage gear on and travel to the school via three bus routes. At best, he could make it for eight o'clock. The school dance started at seven and had to be finished by ten o'clock.

Then I had my brainwave.

'Listen, we can get round this. I'll tell them that you've come from a long way away.'

'But Rick, I only live in Harlesden.'

'Far enough. Just run with me on this.'

He agreed and we were all set.

The week before the dance I worked up the hype about the band, saying that my black American soul singer was actually flying in from Memphis especially for the night. The social context for this is that back then, there weren't that many black kids at school, so making the assumption that he was American was entirely feasible. The schoolkids couldn't believe their luck, the buzz around the school was unbelievable and tickets were like bloody gold dust.

The night of the dance arrived and the deputy headmaster came on to introduce the show. 'Wakeman and his stellar band will be playing for you tonight and I am delighted to announce that one of America's leading soul singers is, at this moment, making his way from the airport to be here tonight. Until then we will be playing records.'

He finally turned up looking knackered but raring to go. 'Yeah, Rick,' he said, 'it's been a really long day – three separate connections to get here.'

Then he got his trumpet out with the Salvation Army logo stamped into it. I tried to cover the logo with my coat and fortunately no one seemed to notice.

As we walked towards the stage, he said, 'Remind me where I'm meant to have come from, Rick?'

'Memphis.'

Cool as a cucumber, he said, 'OK, no problem.'

We went and started playing, our soul singer came on, danced like Little Richard and sang brilliantly and the place went absolutely nuts. He was a sensation. Afterwards, he came up to me and, despite being the star of the show, said, 'Rick, you will make a career in this game, without a doubt. If you can convince a hall full of people they are listening to an Afro-American soul-singing legend from Memphis when, in fact, he is a Salvation Army trumpet player and bus conductor from Harlesden, then you are destined to go far.'

After the triumph of the Memphis soul-singing cameo, there was only one kid the teachers wanted to organise the following year's school dance. And this is where my dad's Standard Ensign comes in.

At a pace.

The problem was, I had lost touch with my bus-conductor friend; after the show, we'd both agreed to play together again but for some reason it had never happened. However, expectations were now so high that the school offered to pay £35 for my band this time around.

This was a lot of money at the time: professional bands were going out at about £20, maybe £25, so this was a small fortune. I sat down with Mr Wright and explained that, with regret, due to the unprecedented number of bookings my band had and the widespread record-business interest, we would normally go out for £50 or more. Which was probably true, had I still got the band, but I hadn't. I'd thought about forming a new one but hadn't actually got round to it.

'Well, we've only got £35, Rick. Can you still play for us?'

'As it's for the school, sir, yes, we'll do it.'

I couldn't believe our luck. Then he asked me the name of the band. I started to splutter. Thinking on my feet I remembered hearing 'Strange Brew' by Cream on some pirate radio station and blurted out, 'Curdled Milk.'

Bear in mind that back then you could buy a slap-up curry for about 50 pence, petrol was about 25 pence a gallon, a pint was 10 pence and fags were 15 pence. Two or three quid gave you a riotous night out. With £35, I figured if I paid the rest of the band £2 each for the night, they'd be ecstatic and I'd be rich.

So I put my band together, with two guitar players, a drummer, a bass player, a conga player, myself and a singer – a seven-piece. Curdled Milk was born. I intended the band to last generations . . . it lasted for one show. Because of rehearsal limitations, all we were going to play this time was twelve-bar rock 'n' roll stuff, but I didn't care, I was going to be more than £20 up.

On the night of the dance, my Ford Anglia wouldn't start. Dad to the rescue, 'Here, borrow my Ensign, son.'

'Brilliant – thanks, Dad.'

I drove to the White Hart pub and met the band for a few drinks. This was just before the days of breathalysers and was not uncommon behaviour. I'd piled my gear in the boot and roof rack of the car and headed off for the school. However, as I'd had a couple of pints and was not that familiar with the rather excellent brakes on my dad's car – compared to the non-existent brakes on my Anglia – I lost control of the Ensign under braking and span it straight across the main lawn at the front of the school, skidding wildly and churning up grass everywhere, until it came to a halt right in the middle of the headmaster's treasured rose garden.

Which was right outside his window.

And was now completely destroyed.

So I'm no longer 'Ricky Wakeman, rock musician', I am 'Ricky Wakeman, lower sixth, shitting myself'. I tried to reverse but, of course, it only churned up more mud. So I put my foot down and tried to go forward, but that churned up even more. Then, in desperation, the guys from the band started pushing me and by the time I parked the Ensign up and looked back at the rose bed it was just total devastation. The lawn was completely wrecked and the rose bed just looked like a compost heap, with mud splattered all up the outside of the headmaster's window. There was a very nice red rose hanging out of the front grille of the Ensign though.

I didn't enjoy the show at all.

For a start, we didn't have a Memphis soul-singing legend with us, or even a bus conductor for that matter. The crowd felt the same and the atmosphere was much more muted than the previous year. But mainly, I was just shitting myself.

Suddenly Mr Wright, the deputy headmaster with the predilection for American soul, walked onstage in the middle of a song.

'Stop, please, thank you, Wakeman, I'm afraid I've got to make an announcement. I'm sorry to have to put a dampener on this evening's proceedings, everybody, but somebody has brought it about themselves to destroy the headmaster's rose bed at the front of the school by recklessly driving a vehicle across it and causing untold damage. If the perpetrator of such a foul deed has the honesty to own up and come and see me now, then I will allow the school dance to continue. If they fail to do this then the school dance will, from this moment on, cease to be . . .'

'Excuse me, Mr Wright—'

'Not now, Wakeman . . .'

'But Mr Wright—'

'Wakeman! If you are worried about your money, you will still get paid.'

'But—'

'Wakeman! Right, the perpetrator has one minute to come forward.'

I stood up from behind my Hohner Pianet and walked up to him at the front of the stage. 'Er, it was me, sir,' I said.

With devastating understatement, Mr Wright paused for a few moments, collected his thoughts and then said quietly, 'Come and see me in the morning, Wakeman.'

I took my dad's car home after the dance, totally dejected. When I got out, I spent the best part of half an hour picking the rose heads out of the radiator grille.

The next morning, they called me out at assembly and ordered me to go to the headmaster's study.

Now I was really shitting myself.

The headmaster, a Dr Evans, was sitting behind his desk looking less than happy.

'Wakeman,' he started, 'I was very fond of my rose garden.'

'I'm very sorry, sir, I lost control, it was my dad's Ensign, you see, and my Anglia wouldn't start and the brakes are terrible but not on the Ensign and I came in and hit them too hard and—'

'Wakeman, you're rambling. Stop. You are fully insured, I hope, Wakeman?'

'Well, it depends what you mean by "insured" . . .' I was still with Cloverleaf.

'Oh, for God's sake. And how many times did you lose control? There seem to be three or four different skid marks.'

'Well, what happened was . . .' I started to feebly explain.

'Never mind, never mind, I don't have the energy to listen. Look, you will have to pay for the damage to the rose garden and the lawn. I have spoken to the gardener already and he has given me an estimate as to what he feels it will cost. Further, you will be banned from bringing your car to the school.'

'It wasn't my car, sir.'

'Wakeman, don't push your luck. Now, the cost of repairs to my rose garden will be £35 which, I believe, is the same amount you were due to be paid for the dance band.'

'That's right, sir,' I said, mortified.

'Well, let's leave it at that, then.'

Except it wasn't so easy for me, was it? I'd promised the band £12 in total and they had played all night, as agreed. So for the privilege of playing a crap gig and destroying a rose garden, I was down by £12. I was gutted. It reduced my post office savings account by half.

They don't make car names like they used to. After the cherished but catastrophic Ford Anglia was sold, I bought a Vauxhall Victor Super Estate, on a 1958 plate. What a name! I bought it out of the *Evening Standard* for £78. It was pure rust. The doors were actually attached at various points with string. There were some parts of the bodywork and interior that had been patched up with paper. It was beautiful.

Then it struck me – the headmaster and the school didn't know this new car was mine. They were still on the lookout for either a blue Ford Anglia or my dad's Ensign. There were quite a few of the teachers' cars in the school car park so I figured that no one would notice me. The first day after I picked up the Vauxhall Victor Super Estate, I drove to school in it. I veered off into the car-park entrance and spotted an empty space. As I drove towards it, I noticed it was next to the headmaster's own car, his pride and joy, a mid-1960s Ford Consul Classic Capri. This, I later learned, was the only thing in the entire world that he loved more than his rose garden.

I lined up the Vauxhall and took my time, determined to park this beauty perfectly.

I was – with the benefit of hindsight – going a *tiny* bit too fast, but nothing ridiculous and besides, the Vauxhall had proper brakes, not like the Anglia. You could stop it on a sixpence. I came in at quite a pace beside the headmaster's car . . .

. . . It would have been absolutely fine if he had not still been in the car and just happened to open the driver's door just as my Vauxhall arrived in the space next to him.

I did, indeed, park my car beautifully.

The only snag was that I took the headmaster's Capri door off with me in the process and pinned it against a wall. I can still see him sitting there, shocked, with the door handle in his palm, looking first at me, then at the ripped-off car door now pinned on this wall.

He got out, brushed himself down and walked off.

Assembly comes and it's, 'Wakeman to see Dr Evans immediately, please.'

'You *are* fully insured, I hope, Wakeman?'

'Yes, sir.' Fortunately, I had moved on from Cloverleaf. But the problem was that this accident had happened on private land, not on a public highway, so my insurance was invalid. Within twenty-four hours my post office savings account had been closed with a zero balance.

'*Any* car you are driving is not allowed to come within a three-mile radius of this school, do you understand, Wakeman!'

This time I did as he ordered.

Although I did drive into his school car park one final time.

Six years later, to give a talk to the sixth-formers on a career in the music industry.

When Yes were Number 1 all around the world.

And I was driving a pure white Rolls-Royce Silver Cloud.

Fully insured, of course. And the headmaster had left his space free for me to park in too!

A BLOODY NICE CURRY

Life on the road.

Good times.

Once you are onstage, anything can happen.

Believe me.

I'm perhaps best known for my work with Yes, but before that band I was in a fantastic outfit called The Strawbs. I joined in 1970 and my year-and-a-bit with them proved very enjoyable and certainly very productive. The media picked up on my performances and magazines like *Melody Maker* even hailed me as 'Tomorrow's Superstar', which was nice. It really propelled me to another level.

In the early days of The Strawbs, however, we played some bizarre venues. In May 1970 we'd been booked to play a circus in France. A promoter had had this brainwave to put on a circus but instead of having the usual big-top band, he'd use various rock and folk bands to accompany the different acts. It was a bit of a cock-up from the start, to be honest, because they got all the names on the poster wrong: Arthur Brown was 'Alan Brown', Heavy Jelly was 'Really Jolly' and The Strawbs were billed as 'Les Strobes'.

The idea was that each band would play for a certain act, depending on the style of music. For example, Arthur Brown played for the lion tamer. I say 'tamer', but to be honest the lion was so drugged up that they had to drag the thing into the ring. When it got there, this lion just wanted to play and he'd roll around a little bit before the climax of the show when the lion tamer forced open the lion's mouth and tried to shove a huge lump of meat down its throat. The very sparse crowd would applaud indifferently at the danger of it all while this lion lay disinterested, meat sliding out of the other side of its mouth onto the sawdust.

We – The Strawbs – played for the child jugglers, the tightrope walker and the man who fell off tables. The child jugglers only lasted five days before they ran out of plates; the tightrope was old, bendy and only about eight feet off the ground anyway so by the time this guy got to the middle he was just walking along the floor; and the man who fell off tables only lasted two nights because during the second performance he fell off a second-tier table and broke his leg.

Now, as I said, this was early days for The Strawbs so money was very tight. We used to earn about eighteen quid a week each from various shows. The circus was having all sorts of financial problems so no one really expected to get paid. I was new to the band, so I was only playing a little electric piano that was supplied for me at the gig.

I had one solo, one tiny little solo in the entire set, which I used to really look forward to. At the end of the first week of shows, we were playing for the tightrope walker and it was coming up to my twelve bars of solo. I was sitting there behind this little electric piano, gearing myself up in anticipation for my lone moment of glory. Suddenly there was a big cheer from the audience and I looked up to find an old man reminiscent of a Roald Dahl character standing onstage waving a stick in the air. Every time he waved the stick, the couple of hundred people watching would roar applause back at him.

Who the hell is that? I thought to myself.

Great.

I had one solo and some weirdly dressed stick insect with a ludicrous moustache from out of the audience had come onstage, started waving a stick and was about to ruin my big moment.

My solo was fast approaching and I was really pissed off, so I stopped playing, walked over and poked this old man on the shoulder. He turned around to face me, complete with curly moustache.

'Get off,' I said.

He looked at the crowd and waved his stick again.

They roared their approval.

I poked him again. 'I said, get off!'

He looked at the crowd again and waved his stick once more.

They roared again.

So I pushed him off the stage.

I went back to my little rented electric piano but by that time my solo had long since passed by and the guys were playing the next piece.

We finished our mini-set and afterwards Dave came up to me looking rather shell-shocked.

'Do you know who that was, Rick?'

'I don't give a toss – he ruined my solo.'

'It was Salvador Dalí.'

'Was it? Really?'

'*Really.*'

'Oh, well, that'll teach him to bugger up my solo in future.'

Sometimes it's not who comes on the stage that is rather un-expected, but *what*. On my travels over the years, quite a few of these road stories have evolved and mutated to the point where the truth is long since lost. They've become rock 'n' roll folklore. Like the time I ate a curry onstage.

I once heard the tale told on the radio that I had a waiter come out onstage with a silver tray and white napkin, serve the curry at a table decorated with a flower and a candle, and then I sat there and ate this meal while the band played on. Bloody hell, talk about Chinese whispers. Or, in this case, Indian.

What *actually* happened was this. It was the *Tales from Topographic Oceans* period in the UK with Yes; as I've mentioned, I was really struggling with the album and tour – there were a couple of pieces where I hadn't got much to do and it was all a bit dull. In those days, I had this great big analogue keyboard set-up and, believe it or not, I used to have my roadie – my 'keyboard tech' – actually lying underneath the Hammond organ throughout the entire set.

There were two very important reasons for this. One, if anything went wrong – which it did on a regular basis back then – he could try and put it right . . . (although he rarely managed to do this. Mostly when something failed he would simply give it a ten-second once-over and announce, 'It's shagged.')

. . . And, two, he could continually hand me my alcoholic beverages.

As I didn't have that much to do we'd often have a little chat along the way; he'd be lying there and we'd talk about all sorts. This one particular night I thought he said, 'What are you doing after the show?'

'I'm going to have a curry.'

'Right, what would you order?'

It seemed a strangely specific question, but I didn't have much else to do so I told him.

'Chicken vindaloo, pilau rice, half a dozen poppadums, bhindi bhaji, Bombay aloo and a stuffed paratha . . .'

'Right.'

About half an hour later, in the middle of the next piece, I was playing along when I started to get this distinct waft of curry. Within a couple of minutes, the smell was overpowering and I noticed it was coming from by my feet. So I looked down and my roadie's lying there holding up an Indian takeaway.

'What's that?'

'Chicken vindaloo, pilau rice, half a dozen poppadums, bhindi bhaji, Bombay aloo and a stuffed paratha . . .'

'What?'

'You said you wanted a curry.'

'No. I said I wanted a curry *after* the show . . .'

'Oh.'

It smelled really good.

I still didn't have a lot to do so I thought I might as well tuck in.

My keyboard tech passed up the little foil trays and I laid this lovely spread out on the Hammond and other keyboard tops. Chicken vindaloo over here, pilau rice next to it, some poppadums over there, a stuffed paratha and Bombay aloo on the Mellotron next to the bhindi bhaji: splendid.

The gig was at the Manchester Free Trade Hall. The Yes faithful had mixed opinions about *Tales from Topographic Oceans* – they either loved it or hated it and that particular night half the audience were in narcotic rapture on some far-off planet and the other half were asleep, bored shitless. But after about five minutes of opening this takeaway the smell of curry started to wake them up.

Jon came over to the keyboards. 'I can smell curry.'

'Yes, I've got chicken vindaloo over here, pilau rice, some poppadums over there, a stuffed paratha in the middle, Bombay aloo, bhindi bhaji: splendid. Tuck in, help yourself.' He took a poppadum and went about his business.

The rest of the band weren't too impressed at the time,

although in later years they did laugh about it. And I tell you what . . .

. . . It was a bloody nice curry.

I very much enjoy playing gigs all around the world. One of the many reasons for this is that many countries have a different attitude towards music – money is not the key motivation like it is in the UK nowadays. Certain countries hark back to a previous time when it was all about the music and it was much more pure in that sense.

Of course, the focus on money has been happening in the UK and America for many years. I'll give you an example. During the early 1980s, I played the Hammersmith Odeon, as it was called back then. We had three electrical systems: one that ran the gear onstage, one that ran the lights and one that ran the PA. This particular night, the one that worked the gear onstage was damaged and we lost all power. For once, this was not my fault – it was the fault of the Hammersmith Odeon. We'd still got a PA and some lights working, but nothing else.

Very quickly, it seemed apparent that there was a major problem which might go on for a while so, keen not to see the audience restless, I wandered up to the microphone and started to tell a joke while we waited for the power to come back on. I remember the joke very well. It was all about a woman stuffing food up her arse and the audience seemed to like it very much.

It went down so well, in fact, that I looked around at the anxious roadies and thought, *Well, I'd better carry on.* I stood there in front of the entire Odeon crowd and continued telling jokes.

Eventually, after forty-five minutes, I heard the sound of a guitar being tuned so I thought, *Great, we're back on.*

We played the show and it went down a treat. Afterwards though, Deal-a-Day Lane came up to me and said, 'That's the most expensive joke-telling session you will ever have, Rick.'

'Why? What are you talking about?'

'Well, we've just been fined £2,000 for going past the venue's curfew by forty-five minutes.'

'That's ridiculous, I was just trying to fill the gap and keep the audience entertained. I bloody well held the fort single-handedly in front of 4,000 people for the best part of an hour. That's not my fault.'

'But Rick, they had the power back on after thirty seconds.'

'PROBABLY BEST TO BOOK IT IN YOUR NAME, RICK'

Celebrity is a funny old game, isn't it? I've been around a lot of so-called 'celebrities' over the years and it always fascinates me how it affects different people differently. Sometimes, particularly within the music industry, it is not so much your celebrity as your *reputation* that goes before you.

Take Alan Yentob, then a producer and director, later to be Controller of BBC2.

Before Alan worked with me, he drank very little, didn't smoke and spoke most eloquently. After two months of filming a documentary with me during my drinking days, he stuttered, smoked forty a day and drank like a fish.

I have apologised to Alan many times for this.

The programme was a series of documentaries called *Success Story*, one of which was about David Bowie and another of which was about me. Alan wanted to feature musical snippets of *King Arthur* and face-to-face interviews with me about my inspirations and ideas and so on. They were really excellent documentaries.

We travelled down to Tintagel, a picturesque village in Cornwall, to do some of the filming as this was supposedly home of King

Arthur's castle (as indeed are at least five other sites). I told Alan that one of my band, namely the singer Ashley, would love to be filmed on a piece of rock jutting out of one of the cliff faces but Alan pointed out that this would require a crane and would create all sorts of logistical problems.

'But Alan, his heart is set on it – is there any way we can do this for him?'

Ashley's heart wasn't set on it at all, as it happens, and I had actually told Ashley that this was something that Alan really wanted to film. Alan duly obliged, and a hoist with Ashley strapped to it was therefore flung out over the cliff face.

Which wasn't ideal, as Ashley suffered from severe vertigo.

Which I knew, of course.

It took Alan four hours to get him back onto flat ground from the cliff face.

They had to call a helicopter and the coastguard.

These documentaries can take months to complete so one of the tricky parts of any production is continuity. For the first phase of filming I'd had long hair, crooked teeth and a beard. So you can imagine which way Alan's blood pressure went when he knocked on my door ready to start the second phase of filming after a two-week break to find that I'd drastically cut my hair, had my teeth capped and shaved my beard off.

Another week of filming was planned for a pub called the Saracen's Head in High Wycombe, where I used to drink regularly. Alan wanted to investigate if the drinking helped my art and performance or hindered it. He'd spoken to the landlord and the people around me and heard all sorts of figures about the volumes I was drinking. Naughtily, I had a word with the barman in advance so, with the cameras rolling, they brought my drink over.

A pint of milk.

'What's that?' Alan asked.

'Er, it's Rick's usual, Alan.'

'Milk? Are you having a laugh? What about all these stories about boozing?'

'Alcohol? Nah, never seen him touch a drop of the stuff.'

Celebrity has changed over the years. When I was sinking gallons of booze daily, there weren't rehab clinics on every street corner. The rehab clinics that were known were mostly in America – even back then, you weren't really, *truly* hip unless you went to one.

I have to be honest, I'm not convinced these places do as good a job as they claim. I'll probably get shot for saying that, but I look upon these places in the same way as I look at a health farm. They both make you healthy in an environment that is utterly unrealistic, surroundings that have nothing to do with your real life. Then, when the people come out, those sterile surroundings are taken away and that's why, in my opinion, so many of them fall off the wagon, because you cannot live that same lifestyle. I think the best rehab should happen out in the real world and not behind closed doors – but that would never work, because the temptation would still be there. I'm not saying you shouldn't go to health farms or, for that matter, rehab, but it's a little like putting your car in for a service. The day it comes out, it runs a treat, but from the moment you pull out of the garage forecourt it's starting to wear out again.

As far as people like Amy Winehouse and the like are concerned, I always think, *Where are the people who are supposed to be looking after her?* Why doesn't somebody who actually cares for some of the young musicians, actors and entertainers coming up through the ranks collate a dossier of rock's fatal casualties in their thirties and forties, and present it to these kids who are screwing themselves up? Hendrix did not have anyone preceding him to look at for perspective or a warning shot; these kids do, there are now several generations of rock stars who have fallen by the wayside. There is no mystery. *We know what happens.*

Unfortunately the one certain thing about the entertainment industry is that it's always been governed by money. Nobody within the industry ever said to me, 'If you keep doing this, you're going to kill yourself.' Why? Because they would probably have been replaced by someone who wouldn't say that and wouldn't stop the drinking and partying. At that stage, you have a certain income status and people, companies, livelihoods are dependent on you. That's why Keith Moon was hauled out of so many scrapes, why Amy Winehouse can leave rehab early and why management mop up these messes and get their charges home in the small hours. You are their income.

It's no good someone like me saying all this, though; when I was that age the last thing I would have wanted was some fifty-year-old lecturing me. But I have to say something, especially when with young ones like Amy Winehouse you see the abyss opening up in front of them and you just take a deep breath.

Ah, Keith Moon. That's reminded me of a great night out I had with him one time. The Who was always my favourite band as a kid – I loved them and still do. One of the great things about my job and my life is that I can now count Pete Townshend and Roger Daltrey as good friends, likewise the late, great John Entwistle.

Moony was a lovely man, he was one stop short of Upney (which, for those of you not familiar with London, is the station before Barking on the District Line), but he just had one of the biggest hearts and I thought the world of him. It is true that he was an incredible drummer, it's not just sentiment. I once said to Roger Daltrey, 'How do you arrange your individual parts when you're putting new pieces together?' Each band does this differently so I was curious. He said, 'Well, Pete and John work out their parts, I come in and do the vocals and then Moony just does a drum solo from start to finish.'

Priceless.

Obviously Keith Moon was famed for driving cars into swimming pools, monstrous partying and suchlike, and we all have our story to tell about a night out with him. I was touring *Tales from Topographic Oceans* with Yes down in Australia at the same time as The Who were playing *Tommy* there, when I had this particularly memorable evening with the man. I hadn't actually known him very long – we obviously knew *of* each other and had bumped into each other after a few shows, but we certainly weren't close friends. So I was pleasantly surprised when my hotel phone rang one evening and it was Keith.

'Rick, I've got a night off tonight. Do you fancy coming out for a meal?'

'I'd love to, Keith . . .' I said with not a little trepidation; my good friend Viv Stanshall had told me that if you went out with Keith Moon, you'd come back either in a police van or via an institution of some kind. This was back in the days when Moony would go out dressed in Nazi gear, goose-stepping into clubs, spraying people at random with a fire extinguisher. So I knew I was lining myself up for something unusual, to say the least.

We met up in the bar and, as we both were rather partial to a drink or seven, got on like a house on fire. Keith said there was a restaurant he wanted to try as he'd heard it was really good.

'Have you booked, though, Keith?'

'Er, probably best to book it in your name, Rick. I'm banned from most restaurants worldwide.'

Keith's reputation at this stage was such that he needed to be this secretive about his night-time forays. We took off in a limo and found ourselves at this really posh exclusive restaurant. It was beautifully furnished and there were about forty tables, all very proper, very formal. The maître d' recognised me and was very welcoming. But when he looked behind me and saw Keith, his face dropped. I introduced Keith – not that I needed to – and

115

Keith just cheekily looked up at this man with that gap-toothed grin of his.

The maître d' paused momentarily: you could almost see him trying to think of a way of not letting Keith eat there, but he couldn't so instead we were shown to a table in the most remote corner of the room. Then he scurried off and spoke with his staff who were obviously shitting themselves over who had just arrived.

However, we ate a delightful three-course meal and Keith was the picture of civility throughout. He thanked the staff constantly, ate his food with great poise, made fantastic conversation with myself, the staff and a few curious fellow diners and was generally the perfect guest. We talked about Yes, The Who, my life, his world – it was a brilliant meal with not a hint of trouble. Keith was the absolute perfect gentleman, stonkingly polite.

When the maître d' came over with the bill, Keith even gently said, 'Can I just say what a wonderful meal that was?'

'Well, thank you, sir. I shall pass on your compliments to the chef. And can I just say what an absolute pleasure it's been having you both dine with us this evening.' The whole restaurant was watching as we stood up from the table to leave and you could slice the sense of communal relief with a blunt knife. I stood up first and started weaving my way through the other tables towards the exit . . .

. . . When I heard this almighty crash behind me.

I swung around to find Moony standing on our table with plates and glasses smashed everywhere. He then proceeded to jump across onto every single table in the room, smashing crockery, bottles, glasses, everything in sight. There was food, wine, stuff everywhere, carnage.

None of the staff ran to the table he was jumping to next, they just ran to the table he'd just demolished. Of course, that meant he was free to destroy every setting unhindered. When he finally landed next to me at the door, he looked up, smiled that toothy grin and simply said, 'Run!'

He lost me within seconds and disappeared into the Melbourne night.

I ran and ran and ran and eventually hailed a cab to take me back to the hotel. Of course, when I arrived there were several police cars already waiting outside. They spoke with me and said that The Who's management had been down to the restaurant and paid for everything and that Keith would receive a formal caution, as indeed did I.

When I saw one of his entourage the next day, I said, 'I'd never been out with Keith before. Does he always do this sort of thing?'

He just smiled a knowing grin at me.

I went down to the pool and there was Keith, on a sunlounger.

The waitress came over to him with a beautiful full English breakfast on a tray. Keith thanked her kindly, took hold of the tray and jumped – fully clothed and with his egg, bacon, sausage and the plate – into the pool.

THE TIN-BATH TECHNIQUE AND THE SMALL-HOURS HOOKER

Prog rock has been much maligned over the years. You have to admit, though, like it or loathe it, we certainly tried to push the boundaries of recording technology. Take the time I had my entire band standing over a tin bath in a cellar, pissing into it.

They don't do that at Abbey Road.

We were at a studio in northern France made famous by Elton John's classic LP *Honky Château* and I needed the sound of a waterfall for a track on the album we were making called *No Earthly Connection*. This was way before the days of samples, so although we had an LP with quite a few water sounds on there they were all pretty rubbish, to be honest – they didn't even sound like waterfalls. We were using a cellar as an echo chamber and, by chance, there was a huge old tin bath in there. I had the brainwave that we should just fill lots of jugs with water and record ourselves pouring this back into the tin bath. We tried it but for some reason it sounded rubbish too – it just didn't work. Plus it wasn't making the sound for long enough. So, over lunch, I came out with the idea that if everybody drank copious amounts of wine until they were desperate for the toilet, but then hung on and on until the very last second, they could all piss into this bath at the same time, making a perfect long-lasting waterfall sound. I reckoned, by my own standards, that we'd have at least a minute's worth of urinating waterfall on tape.

Of course, by the time we'd all drunk copious amounts we were far from sober – a slight flaw in my cunning plan. The resulting tape was nothing short of hilarious. Everyone is sniggering, going, 'Ssshhhh!' and saying, 'Hurry up! Hurry up! I'm bursting!' I was up in the control room, having relieved myself in the normal way in a toilet, in charge of this hi-tech studio wizardry.

'OK, guys, now you've all got to start pissing at the same time, right, it's very important, what we are trying to create here is—'

'Bloody hell, Rick, press the sodding button before I piss myself . . .'

So I pressed 'record' and there was a communal but silent sigh of relief, with an absolute torrent of water gushing into this tin bath. And do you know what? It sounded *exactly* like a waterfall. As time went on, people started to run out of pee and the sound got gradually quieter.

Until there was only one person still urinating.

Martin Shields, my trumpet player.

A further minute and a half went by and he was still going.

The rest of the guys were still all standing around him, flies undone, watching . . .

Two minutes.

Then he stopped . . .

. . . And then started again for about another half a minute . . .

Then he finally stopped.

. . . Only to start again for another twenty seconds or so.

By now, of course, although their bladders were entirely empty, they were all most definitely pissing themselves.

To this day, I still get letters from techies and musos asking me where on earth I got the amazing waterfall sound from on

No Earthly Connection. I simply say, 'All you do is get your band to piss in a tin bath in an echoey cellar in northern France.'

My expertise in studios didn't just extend to sound effects. In 1980, I started work on a new record – to be called *1984* – at Morgan Studios in Willesden. I'd worked there before on various projects, including *King Arthur*, and the studio owner was a lovely fellow by the name of Monty Babson. On this particular occasion we were assigned a really softly spoken engineer who we nicknamed Albert. Now, Albert was about thirty-odd years of age, drove an old Rover and was very much of the old school. A really lovely guy.

A brilliant engineer but not very rock 'n' roll, to say the least.

By way of neat contrast, as a group of individuals we were putting huge amounts of drink down our necks.

Huge.

Each day, Albert would quietly get on with his work and he seemed immune to distraction by our inanities and lifestyle. We couldn't help noticing his reserved manner and he quickly became the topic of conversation. We surmised, through entirely speculative conjecture, that he was almost certainly a virgin and was, in fact, clearly married to his work.

You'd have thought we had better things to talk about. Chaka Khan and Steve Harley were both regulars in the studio, adding their vocals, along with Tim Rice who wrote all the lyrics. It was a real melting pot of global talent.

But the burning question was, *Had Albert ever been given a right good seeing to?*

We thought not and determined to do something about it. Most days started around midday and went on well into the early hours of the next morning as we preferred to work long after midnight – we just seemed more creative and productive that way. On this particular occasion it was getting well into the small hours and

121

there were only three of us left standing: myself, my drummer, Tony 'The Greasy Wop' Fernandez, and good old Albert. Everyone else had gone home, in fact the rest of the studio had been locked up. Albert was still working industriously on some mixes when myself and Tony headed down to the bar to get a refresher. It was left open for us and we just made a note of what drinks we'd taken for the people who ran it to add to my ever-rising bar bill for the duration of the recording.

'So, Tony, do you think Albert's ever been set upon by a woman?' I asked.

'Nope, can't see it meself,' came the reply.

'Well, listen, as a gesture of goodwill and thanks for all the wonderful work Albert has done on this album, I think he deserves a present. Where do we find a woman who can do the honours at this time of night? . . . Hey, I know who will know . . .'

I called my mate Kenny Lynch who I knew would still be up at this unearthly hour.

'Hey, Kenny, Rick here, I need a woman.'

I kid you not, he said, 'What for?'

'Look, it's not for me, it's this friend who hasn't been sorted and we want to give him a present . . .'

'Oh, yeah, sure . . .'

'No, look, listen . . .' And so I explained my idea.

I was then given a number which I duly called and explained to a very pleasant-sounding lady about my friend Albert.

'Look, it's not for me, it's this friend who hasn't been seen to . . .'

'Oh, yeah, sure . . .'

'No, look, seriously . . . my friend and engineer Albert is, how shall we say, a little shy in the female department and he's worked really hard for us recently so as a present . . . you know. Can you help?'

'I will bring someone with me as you're a new customer,' she said, 'and payment is by American Express.' (When it showed up on my credit-card statement, her 'personal services' showed up as a jewellery company in Mayfair, but I certainly didn't buy Albert a bloody necklace.)

In no time at all, a beautiful Rolls-Royce glided up to the front of the studio and a young lady in a fur coat was helped out of the car by this enormous black guy. We went inside and sat down, where I explained that I'd like her to be introduced just as a friend who'd come to listen to the mixes and for her to strike up a little chat with Albert. Then me and Tony could leave and she could, you know, sort him out.

So off we went into the studio and I duly introduced Albert to this woman in a fur coat. He hardly batted an eyelid and politely said, 'Hello.'

After a couple of minutes, I said, 'Er, Albert, me and Tony are just popping down to the bar for a drink. We'll be back up soon.' Turning to the young lady, I said, 'Why don't you sit next to Albert and he will show you what he's doing? That all right, Albert?'

'OK, Rick,' said Albert, completely unaware.

Twenty minutes later, this lady came back down the stairs, by which time we were desperate to find out what had gone on.

I couldn't contain myself. 'What happened? What happened?'

'Bizarre, absolutely bizarre,' she replied. She sat down and proceeded to recount the details of her liaison with Albert.

'I sat down next to Albert and, yes, he is rather shy, isn't he? I gave him a few minutes and then let my coat fall open so that my tits were fully exposed – I have nothing on underneath you see.'

I could imagine. In fact, I already had.

'Go on. What did he do?'

'Well, we carried on going through pleasantries so after a while I just grabbed his balls.'

Tony and me were howling with laughter by this point.

123

'Then I said to him, "What a very nice pair of balls you have, Albert."'

I was gasping for breath from laughing. 'What did he say?'

'In the politest voice possible, he gently said, "Thank you very much, and you have a very fine pair of breasts yourself."'

By this point, the tears were streaming down my cheeks.

'He still made no move,' she continued, 'and I thought we might be there all night, so I pounced on him and had him over the mixing desk.'

Albert duly seen to, the young lady excused herself and left the premises. Tony and myself went back upstairs and walked into the studio where Albert was seated at the desk, working on the mixes exactly as we'd left him.

'Hello, Albert, you OK?'

'Hello, Rick, yes, I'm fine, thanks. Have you known that lady very long, Rick? She's quite forward, isn't she?'

'Er, yes, I guess.' I was barely able to contain my sniggers. 'Anyway, Albert, how are the mixes coming along?'

Without a hint of irony or sarcasm, he said in that quiet voice of his, 'Well, to be honest, Rick, they are a bit jerky.'

My 'relations' with Morgan Studios didn't end that night. The day after the young lady in the fur coat took Albert's virginity, we turned up at the studio but he wasn't there. Most unusual. I walked into reception and the studio secretary – a very nice lady called Pat who ran the place with a rod of iron – fixed me with a grim stare and said, 'Rick, did you have a prostitute in here last night?'

'I did not personally have a prostitute in here last night, no. Why?'

'Monty wants to see you upstairs immediately.'

I went into his office, followed by Pat who said, 'Monty, do something. I know he had a hooker in here last night. Think of the reputation of the studio, Monty. Do something.'

Monty looked up from behind his desk and said, 'Pat, leave us. I need to deal with this very firmly in private with Rick.'

Pat left the room.

'Rumour has it she came dressed in nothing but a fur coat and was an absolute cracker . . . Is this true, Rick?'

'I have to own up, Monty. Yes.'

'Leave me her number and we'll say no more about it.'

I stood up and opened the door. I could see Pat lurking close by. Monty's voice bellowed after me, 'So I hope that's the end of it, and that punishment I've given you will teach you a lesson!'

Pat smiled outwardly.

I smiled inwardly.

About five years later, I heard that Morgan Studios was having some financial problems and had in fact been bought out by another company. I was living in Camberley by then and one day a letter from a solicitor popped onto my door mat saying that I owed the new owners of the studio £6,400. This was 1985, so we were talking about a lot of money. Now, I knew that I had paid all the studio bills fully, there wasn't a note of music from those sessions that hadn't been accounted and paid for. I'd had orchestras and choirs in, all sorts, all paid up. Surely it wasn't anything to do with the hooker business and Monty being so angry? I was completely bemused.

I phoned this solicitor and he explained that there was indeed a debt of £6,400 showing from the 1984 sessions. 'It can't be possible,' I said, and explained how I'd paid for every single note. He didn't have specific details of the debt so I got my accountant on to it, a man called David Moss. He very quickly confirmed that every studio bill had certainly been paid. We informed the lawyer and he set about working out what the outstanding debt was for. About a week later, he phoned me and said, 'Rick, I've finally got to the bottom of all this. The debt is correct and it's from the last eight weeks at the studio, but it's not for studio time . . .'

'Well, what the bloody hell is it for, then? What could I have possibly spent nearly seven grand on in two months?'

'Rick, it was your bar bill.'

The *1984* album also had its fair share of odd live performances. Well, one in particular. As you now know, I get requests from all over the world to play shows, and shortly after this album was released I got a call asking if I would travel to Portugal to promote the record. On the surface, you might think that I'd have been delighted.

However, me and Portugal had a history.

Rewind to the mid-1970s. Border control was complicated: we are talking way before the European Union made it easier to travel across the Continent. And you had to carry paperwork for every border and every country's regulations. So, quite often, mistakes were made. Loads of shows got cancelled and the kids wanting to watch concerts by British bands in particular were starting to get very frustrated and angry. There were even some quite serious riots. Like the time we were due to play to 5,000 in Portugal.

My tour manager Fred had the unfortunate task of breaking the news. 'Not to put too fine a point on it, Rick, our truck with all the gear is stuck in Portuguese customs at the border and isn't going to be allowed out just yet.'

'Well, I'm sure we can speak to the right people and speed it up for tomorrow's show, Fred. How long do they think the delay will be?'

'Five weeks.'

Shit.

Frantic phone calls to the British Consul came to nothing.

'What shall we do?'

'A runner?'

'No, we can't do that – people who've bought tickets will go nuts. We need to think of something.'

Then someone came up with the brainwave of putting an appeal out on radio for equipment. Then, if we scoured every music shop in the vicinity as well, we reckoned we might just be able to pull it off.

The radio appeal went out and, remarkably, by mid-afternoon we had actually got a near-full stage set-up . . . with what could best be described as the leftovers from a car-boot sale. There was some pretty appalling stuff. If I remember rightly, there were a couple of half-decent keyboards and the rest was just ancient, half-working crap. The guitarist seemed happy enough, although the bassist was most disgruntled. There were no monitors and the PA was made up of about forty pieces of unrelated speaker cabinets of varying sizes strapped together which buzzed like a plane going overhead, but it did just about work. If you weren't worried about the appalling lack of any quality.

'What we doing about lighting?'

'I just saw the promoter,' said one of my crew, 'and he said it's all done, something like "No problem, no problem, many, many colours".'

I walked onstage and noticed, above the junk and clutter that was now our gear, a single wire stretched across one side of the stage to the other with about a dozen coloured outdoor Christmas-tree bulbs on it at eight-foot intervals.

I sought out the promoter.

'Err, what's that?' I said, pointing to this festive decoration above my head.

'It's the lighting rig, Rick,' said the promoter.

'Didn't get it from Pink Floyd, did you? Well, how does it work?'

He walked over to a light switch on the side of the stage. He flicked it down and the lights went on; he flicked it up and the lights went out. I realised that I wasn't going to impress the Portuguese audience with a spectacular light show.

We did the gig, all those odds stacked against us – terrible gear, exhaustion, a very confused crowd who were expecting a state-of-the-art performance, and the world's worst light show – and I have to be honest and tell you . . .

. . . It was bloody dreadful.

So fast-forward to 1981 when I was invited to Portugal again to promote *1984* and you can perhaps now understand why I was a little hesitant. Nonetheless, if everything went to plan, I could fly in, do some quick TV and radio interviews, and fly home the next day, having had a nice easy evening out in Lisbon. It sounded like fun so I agreed. But when I got there the whole set-up was completely shambolic. I was having flashbacks and the only thing missing was a set of outdoor Christmas-tree lights.

I did a few radio interviews and then the guy organising the press junket said that I was due to play at an open-air show that afternoon.

'What open-air show?' I asked, immediately concerned.

'Oh, is local event, but live on national radio. About 20,000 people, all very excited you playing a piece from *1984*, Rick . . . The overture.'

'Excuse me? For starters, my band isn't here. Secondly, even if it was, that album has a full orchestra and a massive choir on it. Plus Chaka Khan and some of the most talented musicians and singers on the face of the planet. And I don't sing anyway.'

'Not a problem, Rick – you will be miming.'

How the hell do I mime an overture on my own? I thought. But I resisted the temptation to swear at him. 'How do I mime the New World Symphony Orchestra, the English Chamber Choir and Chaka Khan and my band all at the same time?'

'No problem, we have got you keyboard, Rick.'

One keyboard! Oh, that's all right then. Sorted.

I travelled to the show and, sure enough, there were 20,000 people there. They introduced me very soon after the car pulled up and I walked onstage, smiling and waving at the massed crowd. It was at this point that I noticed there were no other instruments on stage . . . apart from a very small Casio keyboard on a cheap stand, the kind you would buy for a kid's Christmas present.

I had no choice – I couldn't *not* play anything.

So, for six and a bit excruciating minutes, I stood before 20,000 people randomly hitting keys on a £50 keyboard, pretending to actually be playing one of the most complex and sophisticated compositions I had ever been involved with. Then, just after Chaka Khan started singing on the tape and I wanted the ground to open up below me, the compère came on stage and started asking me questions. I have to be honest, I'm normally pretty docile even in the most testing of situations, but for once I was pretty cross.

'So, Rick, you like playing live shows, yes?'

'Not when I'm given a toy keyboard like this to use . . .' I snapped, pointing at the Casio. He turned to the crowd and obviously told them something completely different because they cheered and clapped and shouted their approval.

Backstage after the Casio debacle, I was approached by this chap who said he was from a British submarine crew docked locally and would I like to go out drinking with him and his colleagues. Given my bad experience of the day, I jumped at the chance, not a little intrigued about what life on a submarine was like. I've often been accused of plumbing the depths so I thought this was just one way to find out exactly what that meant.

Bloody hell, they could drink.

We started gently with a solid eight hours. We did have a plate of prawns between us in one establishment, but mainly it was a hard drinking session and I was pleased to be holding my own. The crew were the loveliest guys you could wish to meet and

I've kept in touch with a couple of them. Now, with numbness setting in, I asked if I might be able to board their submarine.

'Sorry, Rick, we're not allowed – HMS *Olympus* is a nuclear sub, you see, there's all sorts of classified material and sensitive stuff on board. We're about to go out on a six-month mission. We're just waiting for the captain to receive his instructions.'

After many more hours of alcohol-drenched revelry, we were walking to the next bar when the crew member on to whom I was holding, as falling over would have been very much an option should I have had no support, said, 'I don't reckon the captain would mind if we sneaked him on for a little look. After all, he's a fan too and he knows we were going to see Rick.' The others nodded their approval. I was about to become a nuclear submariner.

Walking to the port where the *Olympus* was they told me about life below the waves. It was really interesting: they were explaining how most navy vessels changed their personnel on quite a regular basis, but subs are underwater for months at a time and it's a special kind of atmosphere, so the crew hardly ever moved on, and they become quite a tight family.

I should also explain that I had a photographer from *NME* with me who was covering the trip to Portugal. The reason I have not mentioned him up to now is simply because he did not feature – he was an extremely poor drinker and we'd left him where he had collapsed after twelve minutes in the bar we had started in. We went back to collect him on the way to the port. He was semi-conscious but after reminding him of his name and why he was in Lisbon he perked up a bit. I told him we were going on a nuclear submarine and he said, 'Have we missed our plane then?' and fell over.

We literally dragged him off to see the sub. It was way past midnight now and it was the job of the submarine crew to sneak on board one somewhat unsteady-on-his-feet rock musician and a completely pissed photographer. We got to the gate and the submariner who'd approached me backstage said we'd probably get through the security gate with no problem provided I looked like I should be there, so as long as I tucked my hair in behind my collar so that I didn't stand out too much he reckoned it would be fine. I did exactly that and was amazed when we did indeed sail through with a cheery wave from the Portuguese security guards. We walked/staggered over to the sub. She was absolutely magnificent. The conning tower seemed to reach up to the sky. It was one of the most majestic sights I had ever seen. Once inside the submarine, I got the full tour: we walked the entire length many times, I went in the private quarters, the kitchens, the control rooms, I even sat on a bloody nuclear torpedo (it wasn't armed; I asked). Then there was a little commotion and the captain said, 'Sorry, Rick, you gotta go, we've just had our instructions and we're leaving immediately on a NATO exercise.' I later discovered that they were out at sea on this exercise for six months and submerged for most of it.

After I disembarked and watched them sail away I couldn't help thinking about how much alcohol had been consumed over the previous hours, but I assumed that the police didn't tend to breathalyse submarine crews.

Years later, I was doing some promotions for Olympus cameras and was invited to a press day aboard HMS *Olympus*, the very same submarine I had been on which had since been decommissioned. It was moored on the Thames, down by Tower Bridge next to HMS *Belfast*.

The chairman of Olympus cameras said to me on the telephone that this was a great opportunity to see inside a nuclear sub, as so much secrecy surrounded them.

I told him that I'd been in it already.

He said that I must be mistaken. I must be thinking of another non-nuclear sub on Navy Day in Portsmouth or something.

I said, 'No, it was in Lisbon. I was legless and sat on a nuclear missile as well.'

Quite simply, he didn't believe me. He said, 'Impossible,' etc. and that he looked forward to seeing me at HMS *Belfast*.

When I arrived, all sorts of celebrities and dignitaries were there, standing in front of the captain, who was explaining the secrecy surrounding these highly sensitive nuclear vessels. Firstly, he welcomed Olympus cameras and then continued: 'Such is the top-secret nature of these vessels that the strictest clearance has to be applied for even a momentary visit, if the sub is on active service. We know for a fact that other countries have tried on several occasions to infiltrate these vessels so they are guarded with absolute priority. Only a few select submariners and very senior politicians have ever boarded this particular vessel. She has since been decommissioned. You are among a very privileged few who have been invited on board for a tour. We will split the group into two parties, one will come down with me . . .'

Then he looked across at me and with a grin on his face said, '. . . and the notable rock musician Rick Wakeman, who knows this vessel very well, can escort the second party.'

I have never felt so proud in my entire life, as I was aware that every person there was now wondering if I was a rock musician or a spy.

The chairman I had spoken to on the phone was speechless, and as I walked past him I whispered in his ear, 'The name's Bond . . . Rick Bond.'

GONE BUT NOT FORGOTTEN

Sometimes with my job I have laughed until my sides would split; occasionally the opposite is true. I was one of the last Europeans to play in Argentina before the Falklands crisis in 1982. I was down there just before the war started and I had no idea what was going on. The people there had always made me very welcome and I made a lot of friends over the years; there was rampant unemployment in Argentina at the time and a lot of unrest among the younger generation; yet on my return to the UK I already had lots of lovely letters waiting for me on the mat from people I'd met.

Then the war started.

It was very weird for me because I was reading these letters from people who had been at my shows, knowing that some of them would now have been called up to fight the British forces. Worse still, I was living down near Aldershot at the time and I knew friends in the UK military who had been flown out to fight the Argentinians. Both sets of friends loved music, and it was upsetting to think that, in different circumstances, they might have been sitting next to one another at a concert instead of trying to kill each other.

The dilemma for me was that I agreed with Thatcher and felt she was right in what she was doing; for sure the Argentinian government were keeping things from their people, so I had little enthusiasm for them; against that, I really felt the repercussions personally. The thought of two sets of friends being face to face across a battlefield was very troubling to me. So I did what I often do in these situations – I wrote a piece of music. It was called 'Gone But Not Forgotten', an instrumental piece. Tim Rice actually wrote some words for it, but that version was never recorded and it has only ever been performed as an instrumental.

Years later I revisited Argentina for some shows and a woman came to my hotel and asked to see me. I went down to reception and shook her hand. Then she said, in quite broken English, 'Mr Wakeman, I wrote to you, remember?'

I have to be perfectly honest, I didn't recall her letter. I do get rather a lot of mail and it's impossible to remember all of it, obviously. She explained that she had written to me when her son had been serving in the Falklands against the British army. She said she hadn't understood what was going on; she also said her son had been to a show of mine a couple of weeks before he was called up, his last social outing, that I'd signed a record for him and that he'd been delighted by this. She explained how he was very young, seventeen, and very confused and that he'd told her, 'What is going on? The British people are fighting us, but Rick is British and he is my friend, he signed my record.'

Then she told me that he had been killed in action.

It was very hard to know what to say. I admit to feeling the tears well up in my eyes.

Then she held up this bag, carefully wrapped, and said it was a gift for me. She'd read an article about 'Gone But Not Forgotten' and sought out a copy; she told me the music had been a great comfort to her. I thanked her very gently for the gift and expressed my genuine sorrow at her loss. The meeting left a big mark on me.

People in South America give you presents all the time, so I carefully placed this wrapped gift in my suitcase and later that day headed back to the airport and home.

When I arrived home there was a lot of catching up to do with the post and other messages, and so it was a couple of days before I was able to unpack my case. When I opened it up, there, sitting on the top, was the carefully wrapped parcel that the Argentinian lady had given me. I gingerly folded back the paper and opened it.

It was her son's army hat. The tears started to well up again.

Music has that ability to move you. It is a proven scientific fact. One of the charities I have been involved with for many years – the Nordoff–Robbins Foundation – is based entirely on the premise that music can significantly help a variety of disabilities, particularly autism in children.

I've been involved with various charities over the years but this one, set up by two doctors, Nordoff and Robbins, is especially remarkable. Nowadays it's a high-profile charity hosting yearly extravaganzas crammed with celebrities – I believe their annual Silver Clef Lunch is now one of the biggest-earning charity events in the world: it makes millions. I was involved with the charity from the outset after hearing their theories about the therapeutic potential of music.

In those initial stages, back in the early to mid-1970s, they called on various musicians and record companies to get involved and had a great response. When we first started, we needed somewhere to meet. The idea quickly outgrew the A&M offices we initially used, and then they were offered the Moët & Chandon offices just off Sloane Street. At the very first meeting I was somewhat surprised but extremely pleased to see dozens of bottles of champagne on the tables and, sure enough, many champagne-fuelled and, I have to say, very productive meetings followed over the ensuing years.

135

One day I got a call from a man by the name of Willie Robertson, who was a founder member of the charity and boss of Robertson Taylor, which was one of the few insurance companies that would cover reprobates like me and other rock stars. 'Rick, would you like to go to Champagne?' he asked.

I didn't know this was the precise and only region where genuine champagne can be produced. He explained where it was and why I was being asked, as a participant of the charity.

'It is where Count Frederick de Chandon lives and he's invited a group of us to go down there – his family are great believers in the power of music. He wants you to be in that group.' I was delighted and flew down there with great excitement. The count was only about forty and was a splendid fellow, really entertaining and, best of all, he *loved* music. We did all the tours, drank our way through about nineteen miles of cellars – it was phenomenal.

Then Fred came up to me and said, 'Rick, my mother would like to meet you, if you will.' I was more than happy to do so, although I was a little perplexed as to why she had asked for me. He escorted me to the part of the magnificent château where she lived, which was quite a sight. It had God knows how many rooms and chambers, all filled with clearly priceless antiques and period furniture: it really was an impressive country pile. Fred took me into this massive room where his elderly mother was sitting.

'My son has told me all about you,' she said in perfect English with a slight French accent, in the gentlest of voices. 'I hear you play the piano but also the harpsichord. Is that correct?'

'That is correct. I very much enjoy the harpsichord.'

At this point, she indicated a very old but beautifully preserved harpsichord in the corner. She asked if I would like to play it and I jumped at the chance, I couldn't believe my good fortune.

'Well, let's have some champagne as you do,' she said, with a real glint of excitement blazing in her wrinkled eyes. She had had brought in a selection of incredibly rare vintage bottles of champagne. She carefully opened one, filled two glasses and gently sipped hers. I slugged mine back in one gulp.

'That's the last bottle in existence,' she said.

'Nice,' I said approvingly.

I later discovered that at auction that bottle would have been worth in excess of £10,000.

I wish I could remember what it tasted like!

I sat at the harpsichord and played and played. It was an exquisite instrument. Another bottle of champagne was opened and I had a few good slugs but slowed down to more polite sips when I asked her if this was the only bottle left of this particular vintage and she said, 'Rather nice, isn't it, Mr Wakeman? It's from 1896 and is one of only two surviving bottles in the world.' She was half laughing and you could see that my gargling on this priceless bubbly had clearly amused her greatly.

And so I spent one of the most beautiful afternoons of my life, sampling vintage champagnes, eating hand-made nibbles served on a silver platter by a butler, playing a famous harpsichord and talking about life and the world with this delightful lady. I could see that she had a cheeky streak and I have to admit to occasionally pouring the remnants of one vintage glass of bubbly into the start of the next glass, as much to make her giggle as anything else.

'My son tells me that you like history,' she said.

I told her I was fascinated by history and how I believed it is important to understand because it's what shapes our present and our present is what shapes our future, so they are inextricably linked.

'I want to show you something,' she said, returning to her serious self momentarily.

Fred's mother took me through to an antechamber in the middle of which was a huge table covered in maps. 'This is where Napoleon used to come to plan out his battles,' she explained. These were original charts and maps and must have been priceless. I pored over them gleefully for a while. Then she said, 'Sadly, we have run out of time today, Rick, but would you like to come and play the harpsichord again tomorrow?'

Over the next few days, I visited this remarkable old lady and we chatted, sipped champagne and I played the harpsichord. She told me the most amazing stories, particularly about her family's experiences during the Second World War, which really put my showbiz world into perspective. She showed me a picture of her family when she was quite young and – with her voice but a whisper – explained that as they were the most renowned family in the area the Nazis lined up several of them one day and executed them to force the villagers to do what they were told as most of them worked for the family producing champagne.

After that horror, the Nazis forced the villagers to produce champagne for the German army's own consumption and profit. Despite the atrocity that Frederick's mother had just described, that twinkle returned into her ageing blue eyes and with a sparkle in them she leaned over to me and said, with an impish smile filling her face, 'If you ever come across a bottle of our champagne from 1942–44, it's probably best if you don't drink it as you may get a bit of a tummy upset. During that period, some of the French workers didn't always make the trip out of the caves where the champagne was being produced in order to relieve themselves . . .'

After that wonderful visit, whenever I played a concert anywhere for the next few years I would always go backstage to find a dozen bottles of the very finest vintage champagne with a little note from Count Frederick. Sadly, Fred died young and I lost touch with the family, but what an amazing lady his mother was; I will never forget her and I was very sad when I heard she had passed away. I can still hear her now, explaining about the 'special' champagne they had made for the Nazis with that glint in her eye . . .

'Every little thing we could do, Rick, every little thing . . .'

This brings me to another wonderful old lady who adored music, the late Lady Bradford. Her esteemed family was noted for helping to raise millions of pounds over the years for one music-related charity in particular. When she passed away, I was very sombre but my spirits lifted somewhat when I received a call asking if I would kindly play at her memorial service. I was told it was a very casual affair and that there was no dress code. The piece they wanted me to play was 'Gone But Not Forgotten'.

On the day of the service, I was tired but hauled myself out of bed early so as not to be late. I was playing in a charity golf tournament on the same afternoon so, to save time and as it was only a casual affair, I decided to put my golfing gear on beforehand, the idea being that as soon as I'd played my piece I could sneak off and drive down to the course without having to go home to get changed first.

At this juncture I should explain that I like dressing flamboyantly when I play golf, and for this day had chosen a pink-and-lilac patterned golf shirt with a pair of bright yellow trousers with a blue, green and red check. This was the mid-1980s and at the time I was driving a chocolate-brown Rolls-Royce. This beautiful car had one of the very first car phones ever fitted – the equipment and wiring took up most of the colossal boot but I didn't care because I had a phone in the car! It was pretty unheard of at the time and cost a fortune to make calls as well.

Somehow, my early morning start had turned into slow progress and I realised as I was driving into London that time was not on my side. Then my car phone rang – I felt like bloody Batman – and it was my agent, who'd been away for a few days.

'Rick, where are you?'

'I'm just driving into London. Traffic's bad but don't worry, I'm nearly there.'

'Can you get to a Moss Bros?'

'What?'

'OK, listen, I've just been going through the mail and Rick, I thought you should know, there's been a change of plan about Lady Bradford's memorial. It's no longer a casual event, it's very formal, in fact you need ideally to wear a morning suit.'

Shit.

'And they've now got Edward Heath and Michael Foot speaking, several lords are making speeches too . . . there's even royalty coming . . .'

Oh bugger.

'And it's become quite a high-security event, there'll be strict entrance criteria and security presence . . .'

Bugger again.

I explained to my agent what had happened and that even if I could find a men's outfitters there was no way I'd be able to get sorted and still make it in time, and a no-show was out of the question as I had to play 'Gone But Not Forgotten'. Resolving to turn up on time – albeit in my golfing gear – and keep a low profile, I parked the Rolls and headed to the church in Westminster where the service was being held. On my approach, I noticed a side door and, sensing salvation, I forged a cunning plan. I would get hold of Lady Bradford's son, Richard, explain the unfortunate circumstances and suggest that I slide through the side door and get seated at the organ, where I could remain seated and relatively hidden until they announced my piece, which I could then play, and sneak off afterwards. That way no one would be any the wiser about my loud check-patterned golfing trousers. As I got nearer to the church, everybody I saw was dressed either very formally or in a morning suit; I was dressed as Rupert the Bear.

Then I spotted Richard Bradford . . . who had already spotted me.

He was stunned.

I explained my cunning plan.

No good.

The side door was locked for security reasons.

Grasping for a glint of hope, I thought to myself, *At least they'll probably put me near the front, so I can walk quickly to the organ and hide behind it.*

'So where am I sitting, Richard?'

'Right at the back, Rick.'

So there was Rupert the Bear sitting at the back of this church, alongside lords, ladies, politicians and judges.

I was so embarrassed.

At least they might go into my piece quite low-key, I was thinking . . .

. . . And that was when Edward Heath stood up to introduce me . . .

He mentioned how one of Lady Bradford's favourite charities was Music Therapy, how she loved rock musicians and 'always applauded the wonderful work they did . . . one such musician is Rick Wakeman who wrote a piece of music called "Gone But Not Forgotten" which she was very fond of and he is going to perform it now.'

This was the cue for Rupert the Bear to stand up and walk, all the way from the back of the church, slowly, painfully, agonisingly to the front where the organ was situated. It felt like it took me about a year to get there. The silence was deafening, although I did hear the odd whispered comment as I walked by the rows of pews.

'It's obviously drugs,' was one I recall.

The organ was behind a railed fence and when I arrived at the little gate which I had to open to walk to the organ, I discovered it was locked. I shook it, rattled it, swore under my breath at it and then after a minute or so of chronic embarrassment, Rupert the Bear put his leg over and climbed in.

I played the piece and that all went off well. However, there was no way I was going to walk back to my seat, so I just sat there for the rest of the service. Afterwards, outside the church, people in all this formal wear were coming up to me asking for pictures with Rupert the Bear, it was unbelievable. I could see Richard Bradford in the background, howling with laughter; eventually he came over. After what I thought had been something of a debacle, I was really rather worried about what he was going to say . . .

'Rick, thank you so much. My mother would have absolutely loved that.'

THE POLICE WERE
VERY GOOD ABOUT IT

This might sound strange but even though my band was full of mischief, we were never malicious, never hurt anybody or set out to do any harm. Sadly, you do read stories of bands nowadays going around fighting and hitting people, but I have to say we were never like that. We were just very *naughty*. Boys who refused to grow up, who grew bigger, being naughty.

Don't get me wrong, I'm not saying we didn't *offend* anyone.

Take the notorious Snow White and the Seven Dwarfs incident.

On the road, we used to get through almost as many tour managers as we did drinks. No one lasted the pace – at one point we were getting through one tour manager every fortnight. One particular favourite was a gentleman whom I shall call Pat. He was a very good tour manager who once appeared in a double-page spread in the *News of the World* which included a photograph of him with a toilet roll on the end of his knob. He moved into publishing, funnily enough. Very nice chap.

When he was tour manager for the English Rock Ensemble, he worked on the principle that if he could keep the band occupied, then it kept them out of trouble and maybe, just maybe, he might even get some sleep.

On the European tour in question, he arrived in Germany with a Super-8 projector and two films: *Deep Throat* and the rudest animated version of *Snow White and the Seven Dwarfs* you've ever seen. Pure Disney, but . . . er . . . not exactly family entertainment.

Snow White started, as you would expect, with all the dwarfs marching from behind a mountain, singing 'Hi-ho' and all that. Just like the Disney classic. With one small difference, or rather seven rather large differences, as they all had the most gigantic erections. Basically, they all went round to Snow White's house to sort her out, etc., etc. Hi-ho, hi-ho, it's off to bonk they go.

Early on in the tour, we were due to eat at a very pleasant, traditional German restaurant, because we all fancied some Bavarian sausage dishes. It was a reasonably posh place but the staff were very nice and the food was excellent. Pat got the drinks in and was looking very confident that a half-pissed band would behave themselves and eventually roll back to the hotel quietly and fall asleep.

This restaurant was actually made up of two rooms that had been knocked through into one another, and we had pretty much taken over one half of the place. After a few minutes Pat stood up and wandered over to the waiter, had a little chat then came back to the table.

'Listen, lads, I've had a word with the waiter and he's going to let us put a tablecloth up in the space between the two rooms so we can watch my movies, with the sound at minimum volume, if you know what I mean, so it won't disturb the other people eating. I doubt they will understand what's being said anyway as it's in English. After that it's back to the hotel for a few drinks and then we'll call it a day, eh? Sounds good?'

It did, indeed, sound good, so nods of approval all round.

Pat got this enormous tablecloth and started standing on

chairs and taping it up to the ceiling and walls either side, taking great care to make sure that no one else in the other half of the restaurant could catch the slightest glimpse of these highly naughty films. After about ten minutes, his makeshift projector screen was ready and, from where we were all sitting, the rest of the diners would be oblivious to the content of the movies. We were all feeling rather chuffed with ourselves, especially Pat.

'Hi-ho, hi-ho . . .' rang out and we all settled down with our sausages to watch.

Then Snow White appears and starts to get very excitable with these seven dwarfs whose willies are anything but small by this stage.

'Hi-ho, hi-ho . . .'

Next thing we know, there's absolute chaos from the other side of the tablecloth/projector screen, where the rest of the diners are sitting. Upper-class German men are shouting and gesticulating, women are hiding their eyes and crying, it's pandemonium.

'. . . it's off to work we go . . .'

At first we didn't know what was going on, but then the penny dropped.

The tablecloth was see-through.

The entire movie had just projected straight through onto the other side, in full view of the German diners who, like Snow White, were enjoying a bit of bratwurst. The waiters came running over and ripped the tablecloth down, but this made matters much worse, as now the projected obscenities were simply screened on the much larger white walls of the restaurant. Eight-foot dwarfs with four-foot willies were swirling around these walls and I'm sure I saw several women faint (although I'm also sure one elderly German lady called the waiter over to order an extra sausage). Then they tried to grab Pat's projector and he wasn't having it:

145

scuffles broke out amidst the dwarfs and willies and mountains and sausages on the walls, the floor, everywhere.

The police were very good about it.

Breeze-Block Story Number 1: ten days after the Snow White incident, Pat moved on to pastures new. In his place came another tour manager who will have to remain anonymous as his wife, to this day, doesn't know half the stuff we got up to. We'll call him Alex. Anyway, his approach to keeping us in order was very much that of a schoolmaster, the strict disciplinarian.

Talk about red rag to a bull.

'You will do this, Rick, you will do that . . .'

No chance.

Alex was due to fly home one weekend to catch up with his family, leaving on the Friday night and rejoining the tour on the Monday morning. So for the gig on Friday he brought his suitcase, all packed and ready to go home.

Big mistake.

He came into the dressing room and said, 'All right if I leave this in here, gents, for safe keeping?'

A chorus of 'Yes, of course, we'll look after it' all round . . .

As soon as the door closed and his footsteps could be heard fading down the corridor, we sprang into action. We emptied his suitcase and using a combination of sweaty towels and a breeze-block that we'd found in the venue we carefully refilled it so that it felt the same weight, zipped it up and reattached all the airline labels. Previously we'd left stuff like gigantic vibrators and 2,000 ribbed condoms on the very top of the contents of another tour manager's case, but we were particularly proud of our creative thinking with the breeze-block. The crew were always superb at this sort of work. As mentioned before, we even went to great lengths to make sure it weighed roughly the same and then we put it back in the exact same place where he'd left it.

146

For safe keeping.

Halfway through the gig, Alex picked up his suitcase and headed off to the airport. He was due to return after the weekend.

Monday morning came and there was no sign of him.

Lunchtime. Still no sign of him.

So I phoned the office and asked them if they knew of his whereabouts.

'Yes, we do, Rick. They've only just let him out of custody and he wants to kill you.'

'Why?'

'Because when he got to customs in London, they stopped him on a routine check and they asked if anyone had tampered with his case and what was in there, to which he replied, "No, I packed it myself and it's just my personal belongings." When they opened up his case, Rick, they found a breeze-block . . .'

'Did they? Oh dear . . .'

'. . . And promptly arrested him. They took the breeze-block off for forensic testing and kept him in custody the entire weekend. He never even got home. He said he will never work with you again and if he sees you in person he will kill you.'

'Oh, so he's not a happy bunny, then.'

There are certain things you didn't do if you were in a touring band in the 1970s:

1) Fall asleep on an aeroplane. If you did fall asleep, then you did so knowing it was open season for your band mates. Nowadays, with all the restrictions on what you can carry on board, you couldn't get away with this stuff, but we used to have a field day if one of the crew or band took a nap – a particular favourite was to go to the loo and fill a plastic bag with farts, regardless of how long it took (Martin Shields, our trumpet player, was excellent at this as he seemed to be able to produce methane on request – and also when not requested) then return and release said flatulence below the nose of said

sleeping victim. Another top trick was to get a cup of warm water and put the sleeper's index finger in it. For some reason, this will often cause them to wet themselves. It was sheer joy watching the wet patch appear and then waiting to see what they would do when they woke up and tried not to let anybody know what had happened.

2) Never put the slip for your breakfast order outside your room the night before. Fatal. Crew and band members would trawl up and down the corridors to see if anyone had made this mistake. Any slip that was outside a door would be heavily amended with the odd addition to the order.

On one tour in Australia with our orchestra manager Bob Angles we absolutely nailed it. I actually took photographs of Bob shouting at three bewildered waiters who had brought the order on six trolleys. I can still hear him now, shouting, 'Why on earth do you think I would want forty-six sausages? And eleven rounds of toast? And fifty rashers of bacon? I'm in a single room!' The hotel staff had not questioned his ridiculous order because he was the orchestra manager and they presumed he must be ordering for the entire orchestra. The best part was that Bob never actually cottoned on that it was us. He'd just complain about how hotels never seemed to be able to get room service right!

3) Leave your suitcase unattended. See above. Unless you like breeze-blocks and police cells.

4) Leave your key with *anyone*. In America during the 1970s they had a habit of putting elevators on the outside of buildings. You always knew when there was a band in residence because the entire contents of someone's room – someone who'd left their key with a 'friend' – would be put in one of the elevators. Bed, bedside table, wardrobe, mattress, clothes, television, everything.

5) Sleep in a room next door to my singer Gary Pickford-Hopkins.

Why? Well, Gary was a great singer and a lovely guy, who used to play in a band called Wild Turkey. Gary was prone to sleep-walk but, bizarrely, only when he needed to urinate. Apparently this isn't uncommon.

Nor is it uncommon for the person to have absolutely no rec-ollection of this the next morning. My Uncle Peter's favourite place to wee when half asleep was my Aunty Barbara's handbag. With Gary, there would literally be a knock on your hotel door at 3 a.m. and you'd open it up to find him standing there, at which point he would undo his flies in his sleep and piss where he was standing. Sometimes he would actually come into the room, say nothing, and you had to dive for cover as in an open space he could spray it about a bit.

Which, as you can imagine, is a little odd the first time it happens.

Breeze-Block Story Number 2: My choice of builders' materials for my tour managers came back to haunt me during one visit to Holland. I was on a short tour and press jaunt with the PR man from A&M Records, the lovely Mike Ledgerwood. We'd played a great show and then headed back to this little hotel which was right by one of the canals, all very picturesque. The band actually preferred these little hotels to the huge posh chain ones – you might think that they felt more relaxed in the intimate boutique atmosphere of a more petite building, but actually it was largely because they would allow you to drink a lot later and a lot more heavily than you were supposed to. And they'd always be happy to make you a sandwich, which was very pleasant.

This particular hotel had a very nice little courtyard out the back, next to the manager's office, which was made of – yes, you guessed – breeze-blocks. The far wall of this courtyard was decor-ated with potted plants and some trellises and climbers. It was really very nicely done.

I actually took a moment to admire this wall, it was that nice.

Looking back, I should have seen it coming.

That night I went out with Mike for a few drinks. We drank till the hotel bar closed and then Mike said, 'Where shall we go now, Rick?'

'The only places that are going to be open this late, Mike, are in the red-light district . . .'

So off we trotted to the rather less salubrious area of town. We found a suitable 'establishment' and went inside. There was a really nice bar where they were very welcoming and made us feel comfortable, immediately bringing over a drinks menu. Now, these places are not where heavy drinkers tend to go, not least because the general clientele have other things on their minds but mainly because the prices are extortionate. And I mean *extortionate*.

We didn't care, though, and started caning the drink. Not long after, the 'manager' of the establishment came over and asked us if we were ready for him to send some girls over.

'Thank you kindly,' I said, 'but we aren't here for girls . . .'

. . . At which point he looked at how close Mike and I were sitting to each other, immediately presumed we did not bat for his side, and smiled knowingly.

'. . . But it would be very splendid if you could bring over another round. That's all we want and you're the only place that is open.'

'These won't be the cheapest drinks in town, sir. Are you sure?'

'Yes, thanks.'

It transpired that the drinks were more expensive than the women. I didn't mind, it was all going on the record-company expenses! And a receipt for 'Drinks' was going to flag up a lot less suspicion in the record-company accounts department than 'Monica, thirty minutes'.

So we got ratted – we drank shedloads. By 4 a.m., we'd had our fill and asked for the bill, which was stonking. Suitably well oiled, we got a limo back to the hotel where I staggered up to my room for some much-needed kip. My spinning head had hardly been on the pillow for five minutes when the phone in my room rang. It was the hotel duty manager, sounding very irate.

'Mr Wakeman, I would like you to come down to the reception immediately, please.'

'But it's half-four, can't we talk in the morning . . .'

'Please, Mr Wakeman, it is important.'

When I got to reception, a bleary-eyed Mike from A&M was already there. The manager was standing next to him.

'Come with me please, Mr Wakeman.'

Mike and I followed him out to the courtyard. At this point, I was so tired and drunk that it was all beginning to become rather surreal.

The courtyard looked somewhat different to how I remembered it the previous day. The wall wasn't there any more and there was just a long pipe seemingly coming from nowhere with a radiator suspended in mid-air at the end of it.

'I thought there was a wall there,' I said.

'There was,' the manager replied.

He led us out of reception and into the street. The hotel was right by the canal and, sure enough, there was this breeze-block wall. While I'd been out drinking the band and crew had dismantled the wall, removing all the flowerpots and trellises, and had somehow rebuilt it brick by brick out on the bank outside the hotel and in the canal as well.

At that moment, I heard sniggering from the clouds and I turned around, looked up and there were the band and crew pissing themselves laughing from one of the windows.

They weren't laughing, mind you, when we were all standing on the street outside the hotel with our bags at 5 a.m. The final insult was when the manager came out with an estimate for how much the damage would cost – we had a golden rule that if anyone ever did any damage they paid for it personally, it did not come out of the band fund.

When the lads heard the cost, I overheard one of them whisper . . .

'Worth every penny!'

One consistently hilarious aspect of touring is the crew – you get to meet all sorts of weird and wonderful characters. They are first up and last to bed – boy, do they work hard, and do we, the band, reward them with respect and huge salaries?

Of course not.

Let me tell you about one of my favourite crew members, Plug the Roadie.

Whoever you put in charge of the road crew gets to pick the rest of the team. It makes sense, because they'll most likely pick people they are happy with and know will do the job well. Later, through the second half of the 1980s, the technology advanced so much that these guys in the crew had to be supremely quali-fied and it was quite sad because a lot of the old-school roadies just fell by the wayside.

I don't know what happened to Plug in the end, but I do know he was one of the loveliest guys you could wish to meet.

However, he knew as much about roadie-ing as the Pope knows about condoms. I have two cracking memories of Plug. First off, we were on tour and a chap called Big Ian was in charge of the crew – he was very exacting and has since made a big name for himself in the business, going on to be a tour manager for AC/DC and other acts of such profile. He was supremely good at his job. Just to neatly contradict myself, though, Ian had inherited Plug, rather than chosen him. Plug, bless him, could sometimes be a little bit clumsy.

I was walking across the stage at Newcastle City Hall one night, talking to Ian about some technical issue . . .

'So, Rick, one option you've got here is . . .'

Just two out of four things remain in this picture – the cape I'm wearing and me! I've no idea where the chess set is and some tasteless developer knocked down this beautiful house to build a housing estate in the late 70s

I wish I had all these vintage keyboards now! Sadly, many of them went 'walkies' and were never recovered.

I really was the world's worst racing driver. I just didn't have the bowels for it!

I'm guessing this was the 80s …
I mean why else would I look
like this!

This is a very rare photograph
of me with the *King Arthur* keyboard rig.

Well, it was hip at the time.
But looking at it now, I reckon
I look more like a superhero –
'Mothman'!

At Newcastle United's training ground, playing head football with Kevin Keegan.

With a true legend, Eric Sykes.

At Peel golfclub. From left to right, me, Norman Wisdom, Christopher Strauli and Garfield Morgan.

Quite a line up. From left to right, Eddie Hardin, me, Paul King, John Entwistle,
Rick Parfitt, some bloke bending over (if he'd have stood up I could have named him!),
Zak Starkey and Brian Adams (not the famous one!)

Taken after losing my driving licence in 1984.

An early photograph of Yes, where our total weight is what most of us weigh individually now!

Well, it has been said that I'm on another planet!

Chris Squire, Steve Howe, me and Jon Anderson. No idea where Alan is, at the bar probably!

The conning Tower of HMS *Olympus*, with my head sticking out the top.

Me and Janusz Olejniczak in Warsaw.

Another photograph of Yes, taken in the
21st century. And this time Alan turned up!

. . . When a mike stand came hurtling up from the floor area below the front of the stage and hit Ian on the head. Big Ian did not bat an eyelid and just carried on talking to me as if it had never happened . . .

'. . . Or alternatively you could do this . . .'

. . . And as he spoke, he bent down on his left-hand side and seemingly without looking plucked Plug up by his collar. He didn't look at him once, so poor old Plug was just hanging there like a pheasant strung up in a cellar . . .

'. . . It's up to you, Rick,' continued Big Ian. 'Er, Rick, please excuse me a moment,' and with that he thumped Plug on the head with his free hand and then dropped him back off the stage.

Then he turned back to me and carried on talking.

As we walked off stage right, a little voice could be heard coming from down by the photographers' pit . . .

'Sorry, Ian.'

The other wonderful memory I have of Plug is of him during a huge arena tour with Yes. We were working with a very clever man called Michael Tait, a brilliant Australian who had designed some of the greatest lighting rigs in the world. He had to survey the crew as they scurried around these arenas setting up these immensely complicated lighting rigs, like a general watching over his army. You were talking here about eighty crew and an eight-hour build – it was serious stuff. The crews worked eight hours on, eight hours off and all the crews were colour-coded, such as black T-shirts for stage, yellow for lighting, red for sound and so on, as it was such a big operation. Michael would sit perched high up somewhere for the best vantage point and, every now and then, he would shout down instructions and orders, coordinating this massive effort.

It was from his seat with the gods that Michael delivered one of my favourite one-liners of all time. 'Steve, those mikes are too close to the PA; they'll feed back . . . Paul, have we got some more spots for the drums? . . . Geoff, Geoff, can we run a test on that guitar? . . . and Plug . . . whatever you are doing, it's wrong.'

One of the things I always did, and still do, before a tour started was take the band and crew out for dinner. For my 1984 tour, when we were all done rehearsing we headed for the Warwick in Maida Vale where some fairly heavy drinking ensued.

I'd love to know the connection between drinking too much and that neon sign in your head that says 'MUST EAT CURRY'. It's amazing, isn't it? Well, that was what happened, so all twenty or so of us went off to this Indian restaurant round the corner. They very kindly pushed all the tables together, even though you could see they were more than a little apprehensive about what we might get up to.

The waiter came over and asked if we were ready to order.

'Yes,' I said. 'To start with we'll have two hundred poppadums, please.'

They brought these poppadums in on God knows how many plates – it was like *Record Breakers* with Roy Castle or something, it was hilarious – and put these teetering piles of crockery on the table. Then they retired quickly to avoid having to take the actual main-course order.

'How are we going to break these up, lads?' someone piped up.

The next thing I knew, Ashley stood on the table, dropped his trousers and whacked his old chap on one of the piles of poppadums, sending bits flying everywhere and causing absolute uproar.

Within seconds we were all down to our underpants.

The police were very good about it.

'The restaurant owner wants you to pay for the damage.'

'What damage?'

154

I thought the only damage might have been if Ashley had scratched his old chap, but I decided it was best not to mention that to the policeman.

Life on the road.

Good times.

'HAVE I DONE SOMETHING WRONG HERE, GENTLEMEN?'

Eastern European composers are absolutely my favourites. The greats, such as Prokofiev in particular, have always held a fascination for me. It wasn't just their Eastern European composers' incredible music, either: their own stories were compelling too. Take Chopin. After he died, his heart was cut out at his own request because of his fear of being buried alive. It was then taken back in an urn to Poland by his sister and placed in a pillar of the Holy Cross Church in Warsaw. So they say that although Chopin died in France, his heart will always be in Poland.

Which is rather lovely.

Although not the bit about cutting his heart out, obviously.

So you can imagine how delighted I was when I was invited to Poland to work with Janusz Olejniczak, one of the country's finest pianists. The Frederick Chopin International Piano Competition is one of the oldest piano competitions in the world. It started in 1927 and has been held every five years since 1955. The competition attracts the very finest pianists from around the world. It really is a magnet for the absolute elite players. For someone like me, those competitions couldn't really be any more amazing. So to be asked to work alongside a winner of this prestigious competition was a dream come true.

Some context is needed here. This was 1982, before the Wall came down and certainly before the Eastern Bloc had opened up to the West. The height of Polish problems, in many respects. Cracks were showing, however, and young people in Poland were starting to get hold of Western press reports, the occasional smuggled vinyl disc or articles of the latest fashions. Although this was pre-Internet, communication was nevertheless improving at such a rate that it was getting less and less easy to maintain state control. In a vain bid to satisfy this exploding interest in all things Western, the Polish government came up with various hare-brained schemes, one of which was to get a Western pianist to play alongside a famed Polish musician to produce classical music with an electronic overtone.

Which was where I came in.

I was approached by an agent called Rod Weinberg who said my name had come up in conversation for this very task and would I be interested? I couldn't say 'Yes' quick enough. The main reason I seemed to fit the bill was because although I had enjoyed commercial success in a 'Western' rock band I'd also had a full classical training culminating in two years at the Royal College of Music and had worked with major orchestras around the world.

So in the cold winter of 1982 I found myself on a plane to Warsaw. My first impression was it was bloody *freezing*! I can still feel the cold in my bones now. I quickly scurried into the shelter of the main airport terminal where the temperature gauge registered minus 25 degrees, and joined the back of the queue for customs.

Two hours later, I got to the front of the queue.

You had to list everything you had with you, everything in your case, even everything you were wearing, down to buttons missing and so on. It was insane. And all this after I'd been invited to go there.

Once again, Harry Palmer kept flickering across my mind.

Eventually I got through customs and was met by a man called Yachek, a government official charged with looking after me (a task at which many world-class tour managers had, as you now know, failed abysmally). He instantly seemed a very pleasant albeit slightly reserved man, and we chatted along merrily. I could see he wasn't an 'ordinary' worker, because he stuck out a little bit from the crowd: his clothes were a little Western in style, slightly better quality than most and with richer colours. Most obviously of all, he drove an old Ford Escort that was, quite frankly, falling apart – perhaps only slightly more road-worthy than my beautiful old Ford Anglia. That might not sound like a Howard Hughes standard of wealth, but in Poland very few people owned cars, you hardly saw one on the street, and of those nine out of every ten cars were very old, very battered Ladas, Skodas or Trabants. So driving this Escort was like rolling around in a Bentley. It was the best car I saw during my entire stay in Poland, by some considerable margin. It has to be said though that the old Ladas started first time every time in all sorts of unbelievable conditions so the bad name they got in the West is actually unfair.

Yachek drove me to a fairly dishevelled hotel that was used exclusively by visiting Western businessmen – not by any members of the general public – so locally it was considered quite upmarket. I was immediately struck by how *grey* everything was: the buildings, the clothes, the cars, people's skin, everything. The street lighting was very low too, almost like either the energy was running out or there wasn't the money to keep them on brighter. Perhaps it was both.

159

On arrival, I was checked in swiftly and taken to my sparse and very basic room. It had a small bed, a tiny shower room with a shower-head that, at best, dribbled water out at you feebly. The decor was . . . grey.

The rooms were almost certainly bugged. I told Rod Weinberg this (he had travelled with me), and about this time in Russia where in one of the few very sparsely decorated rooms I was staying in I said out loud to myself that it would be nice to have an extra bath towel – and five minutes later there was a knock at the door and a woman stood there with a bath towel in her hands to give me. Rod thought this was highly amusing and walked into his room saying in an extremely loud voice, 'Don't think much of the colour of this carpet!'

Nonetheless, I didn't expect anything else – and besides, on our way to the hotel I noticed we passed Łazienki Park where the memorial statue to Chopin had been erected just before the Second World War. Every Sunday, in the warmer months of the year, musicians performed free piano recitals of his work next to the statue: it was a renowned and revered focal point for Chopin fanatics and pianists around the world.

I was desperate to go back to the park straight away.

Unfortunately, Yachek had said to me in reception that I was not allowed to go anywhere without him, under any circumstances. His room was just down the corridor and he insisted I could knock on his door at any time of the day or night, as long as I did not leave the hotel alone. A meeting with Janusz, this famed pianist who I was to work with, was arranged for just after breakfast the next morning.

I slept fairly fitfully that first night and woke very early from the hard bed. It was only 5 a.m. There was no breakfast place if I recall and I was keen to see what was happening outside. The room was virtually empty – certainly no television – so there was absolutely nothing to do.

I thought, *I'll go to the park and look at that Chopin statue.*

I knew I'd been told this was exactly the sort of thing not to do, but I wondered what harm could it really do? It was still half dark outside and I walked through the small, empty hotel foyer without a hitch, straight out of the door and into the forbidden streets. There was no one around. I saw only a couple of people fleetingly. The odd tram, a Lada, a cyclist.

Remembering the biting chill, I'd wrapped up heavily and had used the scarf to hide my face. The tiny strip of my eyes and forehead that was exposed to the cold was frozen within seconds. I remembered the way to the park as it wasn't that far from where we were staying, so I walked there but the gates were closed.

Bugger.

Then it started to snow.

Bugger.

It was so cold that my feet, inside my woollen socks and fleece-lined boots, were frozen solid.

There was no one around at all now, so I climbed over the gate.

I was so desperate to see this statue and the stage where people played that I wasn't going to let anything get in my way. I'd seen pictures; if you are a professional piano player you know what it looks like, but I wanted to *see* it for myself. I stood in front of the statue, soaking up the history, when I suddenly became aware of two figures standing just to my right.

'Hello, Mr Wakeman.'

It was strange, because as a musician in various well-known bands I'm used to strangers saying, 'Hey! Rick!' and all that; yet, here in Poland, there was no reason to expect this, not least because my own mother wouldn't have recognised me in the secretive scarf and hat.

They spoke perfect English. But they weren't from England.

'Hello,' I said, almost by reflex.

'My name is Boris and this is Ivan,' the tallest one said.

You're having a laugh, I thought.

He wasn't.

'It's very early and very cold, Mr Wakeman. What are you doing in the park?'

'Well, it's funny you should say that. I woke up really early and I'm supposed to be having a meeting later with Janusz Olejniczak about working with him, mixing wonderful Chopin works with some electronic keyboards, but I woke up early and, being bored, thought I'd come and look at this famous landmark. The gate was locked so I climbed over it. How did you get in?'

'We have a key. We would like to take your photograph.'

'Great,' I said, relieved. 'I'll stand by the statue, shall I?'

Out of his large trench coat Boris produced a really old-school camera with a detachable flashbulb, like something Prohibition-era paparazzi would have used. He took a picture of me staring directly into the camera with the statue right behind me. He looked a little close to me but I wasn't about to complain.

'And would you like to turn ninety degrees to your right and I'll take another picture, Mr Wakeman . . . ?'

I did as I was told . . .

'And now 180 degrees please, so you are facing the other way . . .'

It was only at the last second that I realised what he was doing.

'I've done something wrong, haven't I?' I said, with a growing sense of unease.

'It's OK. Please follow me.'

I didn't really have much choice so I did, indeed, follow

them. At the park gates, Yachek's trusty old battered Ford Escort was there and as he saw me he got out of the car. Like my friends Igor in Moscow and Barry the Perv in Paraguay, he was as white as the snow falling on the ground. I seem to do that to people. Ivan and Boris didn't shout at Yachek but he was given a very firm talking-to.

In Russian.

Eventually, Boris came over to me and said, 'Enjoy the rest of your stay in Poland, Mr Wakeman, but please do not go *anywhere* without speaking to Mr Yachek first.'

'Thank you very much. I hope I haven't got Mr Yachek into any trouble. I was only coming to see the statue.' With that they left and I climbed into the Escort, suitably chastised.

Yachek looked quite cross but very politely said, 'You're not allowed to go out on your own – I told you this, you mustn't go anywhere on your own. Please. I get privileges. I have an apartment just for me and my family, I have a stereo and a television and I have my car. I can lose all of that.'

I apologised profusely and felt awful.

'Who was that, by the way?'

'Russian. The KGB. Their embassy is almost directly opposite. They still monitor everything we do.'

After that brush with the Russian secret service, everything went relatively to plan. I went back to the hotel and met Janusz and we talked about Chopin and Western music and how we could make something new from these various influences. I came up with the idea of making something suitable for a string quartet.

'Yes, they will like that,' said Yachek.

I wasn't sure who 'they' were, but Yachek then offered me any musicians I wanted, so I didn't really care. He also said any venue and any orchestra would be made available, as would any recordings we might need. There was one big problem, though – they didn't have any electronic instruments which, when you are trying to write an electronic/classical collaboration, can be quite a sticking point. So, in other words, they gave me everything except the one thing I needed. I also couldn't ship any keyboards to Poland at that time, as to even try and consider getting the paperwork was nigh-on impossible and whilst musicians, manpower, recording facilities etc. were free, there was no hard currency budget to get in equipment.

While I worked on the music with Janusz, I was also invited outside the city to various houses that belonged to other renowned musicians and local dignitaries. Janusz was also enjoying some privileges and he invited me to his apartment and also to his parents' house. I remember going to one small house belonging to a friend of Janusz and the table was laid for one person with a plate on which was beetroot and salad and a pig's trotter. In many of these households, if there was any meat available it was pig's trotter. Nobody else ate. I was shown to the single chair where I ate everything; it was obvious in certain cases that I was getting the best food they had in the house, so not eating it was not an option, out of simple courtesy if nothing else. These people were in the depths of poverty and yet would have given me their last grain of rice to make me feel welcome. Very, very proud people, lovely. To this day I have a wonderful warm feeling towards the Polish people. They are some of the kindest and nicest folk I have met on my travels.

One particularly fascinating character I met was Janusz's father-in-law. He was a publisher, so he worked with the authorities on what was and wasn't allowed to be printed for public consumption. He worked in a magnificent oak-lined office – a throwback to Mervyn Conn from all those years ago! Next to his room was a receptionist's room, just like at Mervyn's.

But we couldn't have been in a more different universe to Leicester Square.

I went into his office and, once again, there was a mysterious man in a suit joining the meeting. It was blatantly obvious that I was not going to be left on my own anywhere in case I asked anything I shouldn't ask, or said anything I shouldn't be saying or was told anything I shouldn't be told. We had weak tea and talked generally about music and books. Already, in a few short days, I'd learned to be very careful about what I said and what I didn't say.

As I was leaving, the publisher said to me quietly, 'It would be nice if you came back soon. Come back and have tea with me tomorrow, before you go home.'

I did exactly that and, for some reason, we were alone this time.

Yachek, who had accompanied me as usual, began to pale.

The publisher asked me into another room on my own.

And that's when Yachek went a whiter shade of white.

As the publisher closed the door, he said, 'What do you know about Warsaw?'

'A little more than most, but a lot less than many,' I answered honestly. 'I know the tragedy of Warsaw at the end of the war when the Russians obstructed Polish resistance efforts and in effect allowed the Germans to burn the city to the ground.'

'Do you know about the band of child soldiers, Mr Wakeman?'

He then proceeded to tell me about these child soldiers who lived in the hundreds of miles of sewers below Warsaw and formed some sort of resistance. There are statues *in memoriam* of these poor kids and it was very moving to hear the tale told by such a man. The Russians couldn't track them down in this extensive and antiquated sewage system and couldn't blow them up because it would destroy the waste

165

system for the city. Then he showed me a book of photographs, a pictorial chronology of exactly what the Russians and Germans did to Warsaw at the end of the war. I hasten to add that what the Allies did to Dresden was no less inhumane and it does seem that war has no love for people, history, art and beauty. I remember speaking to an American astronaut friend of mine not so long ago who said that every world leader should go into space and look down at the earth, which becomes just a tiny speck among millions and millions of other tiny specks, so they can realise that our tiny speck is the only known place in this universe with life, and then perhaps they would think differently about slowly destroying it, as all world leaders seem intent on doing.

Back to the oak-panelled room: 'Never ever underestimate the Poles,' he said to me. 'If someone said there were cabbages available, there'd be a two-mile queue. The last people in this two-mile queue would wait patiently, knowing that there would almost certainly be nothing left when they got to the front. But they'd wait nonetheless. If ever the opportunity arises, you watch Poland rise: we are the hardest-working people you will ever meet.'

I couldn't agree more. If you kept animals in the way that some of the Polish people were kept back then, the RSPCA would take you to court.

I couldn't help but think that, at that time, Poland was in the worst possible geographical sandwich: East Germany on one side and Russia on the other. It was so sad. A few months after the Wall came down, I went back to Poland, which now had a Western border. The change was unbelievable. My friend, the publisher, was right. 'Watch the Poles rise,' he'd said . . . and they certainly had. They had embraced their new-found freedom with hard work and creativity. I take my hat off to them.

As I was about to leave the company of this amazing man, who had so many stories to tell sitting in this oak-lined office, he leaned over to me and whispered in my ear . . .

'Mr Wakeman, please do not speak a word of this to anyone, but I was one of those children . . .'

'NO, MR WAKEMAN, SIX MONTHS TO LIVE'

You remember all that medical advice after I'd had those two heart attacks? And do you remember how I didn't actually heed any of it? Well, let me tell you how I finally came to stop smoking and drinking.

Initially, my heart attacks and degenerative ill health had very little impact on my choice of lifestyle. As you know, against all medical advice I travelled uninsured to America to tour *King Arthur*, had a jolly splendid time and underwent more ECGs than the Bionic Man. I have to say that when I came back from the States I was feeling really, really good. I had laid off the drink a bit and I had cut down the smoking a lot. I phoned up Jess Conrad, who organised matches for the Top Ten XI football side (which I'd previously been a keen member of) and asked him when the next match was.

'Are you sure you're well enough, Rick?' he asked.

'I'm fine, yes.'

I played the game and scored four goals.

I have to be honest and say that it was as much down to the other players as me; you see, it was common knowledge that I'd had heart attacks and been really ill. So on the day of the game, no one would come near me, everyone was terrified to tackle me. At one point, for no particular reason, I did get banged up in the air and came down with quite a crunch.

You've never seen twenty-one men panic so fast.

I was lying there gathering myself to get up and all I could hear were these whisperings of '. . . heart attack?' or '. . . still breathing?' or '. . . ambulance?' Someone came right up to me and said, 'Shall I give him the kiss of life?'

'I've only hurt my bloody elbow!' I roared, laughing and wincing at the same time.

Not long after the game I had to go to Harefield Hospital for another of my regular check-ups. Even though I was progressing well I still had to be closely monitored. On this occasion the consultant hadn't seen me before and seemed not to know about my recent jaunt in the States. He started asking me the usual stuff.

'Mr Wakeman, your ECG is good, your blood pressure's fine, it's all excellent. I can see you've been taking it easy and heeding our advice. Good.'

'Well, er, not exactly. I've just come back from a lengthy tour of America.'

'Oh, I see. But *otherwise* you've been taking it easy?'

'Well, sort of, although I played a game of football last week.'

'Remarkable. There's no scarring on the heart, everything looks great. Obviously the pills we gave you are working perfectly.'

'I wouldn't know. I ran out of them six weeks ago.'

They discharged me completely three months later.

As you know, I did give up cigarettes but only because I'd moved on to cigars. The doctors were horrified. Smoking was a real concern for the heart. They said I obviously drank too much but, 'For God's sake, stop smoking, Mr Wakeman!' I tried and I tried and I tried. The New Year's resolutions came and went but could I even last until Lent?

Not a hope in hell.

Then a bizarre thing happened.

We were on tour with Yes in 1979 and had a break from the road in October. As I often did during a prolonged period of time off, I rented a house in California to relax in. It was pointless flying home because by the time I'd got over the jet lag it was time to fly back again.

Mornings in my West Coast retreat were particularly robust on the flatulence front (more about that later). A veritable cacophony of sound and smells. On this particular morning, I was sitting at the table enjoying my usual breakfast of a Café Crème cigar and a large, strong cup of coffee (my first of ten such each morning). I opened the cigar tin, looked down at the little cigarillos . . . and for some reason I do not know to this day, I thought, *I really don't want to smoke any more.*

And that was it.

I stopped smoking there and then.

October 1979.

Even more bizarrely, I have never had a single withdrawal symptom, not one. Years later, I might unearth a cigar tin from the back of a cupboard and I'd just look at it and throw it in the bin. There has never been any chance that I'd go back to it.

The habit's persistence is incredible to me because there are billions spent on anti-smoking campaigns, nicotine patches, hypnotherapy, counselling and all sorts of wonderful, energetic remedies for the curse of smoking.

But really, in my experience, the process of quitting is really very straightforward. You have to want to. If you don't really want to, then all the patches, creams and tablets in the world won't help you.

So now it's time to tell you how I gave up the drink. I suspect many of you will be skimming through this section in your eager-ness to get to the flatulence story I promised you, but I shall continue. Despite having had two heart attacks and numerous health repercussions due to my excessive boozing, I still drank like a fish. By the mid-1980s my capacity was still legendary, you couldn't put a price on it. Well, actually, someone did.

I knew a lot of journalists in Fleet Street and often saw them at a famous pub called the White Hart, which was better known as the Stab in the Back. It earned its rather gory nickname because the only time an editor would take a journalist there was to give him the sack. There was a little eating area on one side, so you knew that if your boss said, 'Hey, let's go down the White Hart for a bite to eat,' then that was the end of that.

It was an old-fashioned pub just off Fleet Street, a perfect journalistic time warp with old-fashioned reporters' phones all along one wall. I used to sit in there and meet some great people. Frank Dickens used to draw the Bristow cartoons for the *Evening Standard* and he'd regularly be in there. He once did the most amazing cartoon of me on a napkin, as quick as you like. You'd be sitting drinking with him and a girl would rush in from the editor's office asking him to file his drawings urgently for deadline. Frank was a serious drinker and, on more than one occasion, I actually saw the girl Tippex out the beer-glass rings on his drawings before she scurried off.

There were loads of characters like Frank. I was one of the few outsiders to the journalist profession who was welcome there, so I got to know many journalists and in later years that's how I found out that there was a price on my head.

The deal was, any journalist who knew me and could take me out drinking and *actually get me pissed* would win £100 and two bottles of vintage champagne.

Many tried, all of them failed.

I very quickly lost count of the number of sozzled journos I left propped up semi-conscious at the Stab in the Back. I've often thought about my alarming capacity for drink and I think it must be something to do with my DNA make-up. This idea is reinforced by the fact that I didn't actually get that drunk, I would never stagger around legless. I could go out on a really heavy session and talk coherently all through the night and then walk home. My theory is further reinforced by the fact that until I became ill in the mid-80s *I never got hangovers*. I could go out and, literally, drink a plane dry, then wake up in the morning with no hangover what-soever. I might occasionally feel tired, but that was from being up late and was nothing that a good strong cup of coffee couldn't fix.

It was later explained to me that both these unusual abilities – to not get that drunk and to never suffer a hangover – were actually part of the problem. That's because they are both ways of your body telling you to stop. Being drunk and all the head-swimming, leg-wobbling nausea that comes with it is simply your body being unable to cope with what you are putting into it and it gets alarmed: the signals are pretty obvious. Likewise a hang-over has put many a drinker off continuing. Not me. And that might seem funny for a while, but actually it was all part of a lethal cocktail of circumstances – drink, excess, exhaustion and bad health – that nearly killed me.

I class myself as lucky to still be alive. Let me share the legacy of excess I can 'boast': amongst numerous self-inflicted health issues, I've had alcoholic hepatitis, chronic pneumonia, double pneumonia, pleurisy, legionnaires' disease and heart attacks.

Nothing to bloody boast about, I know.

I have really pushed my luck.

I'd given up smoking in 1979 but it wasn't until 1985 that I finally gave up the drink. I think there is no doubt that I prob-ably wouldn't be here if it wasn't for that. The drink was the worst problem.

At one point they gave me six months to live if I didn't stop. That did the trick.

If fear gets hold of you it can be the greatest doctor you could wish for, and the greatest counsellor. I was an astonishing drinker

– I used to drink port and brandy in pint glasses: half a pint of port and half a pint of brandy in a pint glass, that was 'my' drink . . . with beer chasers. I'd drink phenomenal amounts of beer, wine, port, brandy, all sorts. Of course, it caught up with me in the end and, when it did, it was like being run over by a juggernaut.

I was in Australia and started feeling unwell. Up until this point I had felt fine, it sort of came out of the blue. I couldn't keep any food down, I kept suddenly falling asleep in the middle of the day, my skin had this awful yellow pallor, I couldn't always control my bodily functions and I was losing weight fast. I could tell that my organs were basically stopping working – the pancreas, the liver – my body was shutting down, my innards were collapsing. It was obvious that I was really ill.

When I came back from Australia, nobody recognised me because in three weeks I'd lost three and a half stone. I had a doctor friend in Harley Street called David Myers so I went to see him and explained my symptoms. Without even examining me, he said, 'Rick, I know exactly what is wrong with you. You have alcoholic hepatitis, I'm afraid, as well as all sorts of other problems probably. I'll do some blood tests and a full examination and see what's working but we may also have to set up a biopsy.'

When the results came through, he explained that my liver function was severely depleted and my kidneys were equally suffering.

'But they are still working, aren't they?' I said, my ignorance making me feel almost positive.

'Yes, they are, but they will continue to deteriorate, I'm afraid, unless you take drastic action. The good news is that some organs are actually regenerative, so in time you might be able to make a near-full recovery. But if you don't do what I tell you *today* the consequences will be critical. You have to stop drinking otherwise the downward spiral will continue.'

'So what do you think, then?'

'Six months.'

'OK, no drink for six months, I can do that.'

'No, Rick, six months to live. Unless you do what I say. And if your functions drop below this line here,' he said, pointing at a graph, '. . . maybe less.'

I was struck dumb.

I was absolutely shitting myself.

This was 1985 and I was only thirty-six.

'Your drinking days are over, Rick. They are absolutely one hundred per cent over. You will need to follow a strict diet plan, and you will need to come to see me weekly at first, for pretty much constant monitoring. I cannot promise you that you will come out of this, even if you take my advice. For starters, you will experience terrible withdrawal symptoms that in some cases have been known to be fatal themselves. However, if you don't do what I say I can promise you that you won't be around for much longer.'

I was due to become a dad again in eight months' time and it was quite chilling when he said, 'I have to be honest with you and tell you that you may not live to see him.'

He didn't need to say anything else.

I walked out of the clinic, right down York Street and into a pub called the Duke of York, a favoured haunt of The Strawbs in the days of some very heavy drinking sessions. The barman knew me well and, naturally, he asked me what I wanted to drink.

'A tomato juice, please.'

'OK. Had a hard night boozing, Rick?'

'No, I don't drink any more.'

I was never the type to 'cut down'. I had to stop completely, just like Dr Myers said. He also gave me a list of names he said I'd need to get help from for the incredible withdrawal symptoms including AA and other rehab places.

But do you know what?

I never had a single symptom, not one. Just like when I gave up smoking.

Nothing: no shakes, no hallucinations, no sweats, nothing. (Barry the Perv still sweated more than I did, just from being a perv.)

People ask me how that can be and I put it down to fear. I'd never been so terrified in my whole life and I've been close to the old Grim Reaper on a few occasions, let me tell you, but my condition was totally self-inflicted, the closest thing to medical suicide. After a while I'd recovered enough for the six-month prediction to have evaporated, but I could still become incapacitated enough to stop me working in the long term. The climate of music at the time was not particularly generous to the likes of me, but I didn't care, I just loved playing. I remember one day after I'd been to see Dr Myers I went back home and played the piano. It was *so* enjoyable and I thought to myself, *Do you really want to lose this? To lose what you love doing, being creative, making and playing music?*

Eventually my organs started to work again as they should; it's a remarkable thing, the human body. Incredibly, despite my awful history, I recently had a medical which showed that in my late-fifties I am actually fitter than when I was in my thirties. I'm extraordinarily fortunate.

I think that when you are in your teens and your twenties and even your thirties, the word 'death' is not in your vocabulary. On the odd occasion it does crop up, it's usually a granny or an old aunt or, if you are unlucky, someone who's been in an accident. You do not associate death with your life at that age. That is reflected in what you do to your body – in my case I gave it a complete battering. You drink to excess and maybe smoke like a chimney, even though you know that both activities are killing you. You're not stupid: you've read all the articles and seen all the bulletins. But you do it anyway. It's when you hit your forties – and then definitely your fifties – that death becomes a little more relevant and very frightening. Fortunately for me, by that stage I was long since recovered. Sadly, that's not always the case for many of my peers. I saw one survey claim that the average life expectancy of a rock star is forty-six. That sounds very low but I do know that there is a huge list of contemporaries and friends of mine who aren't here any more.

My saving grace was never having taken drugs. One of the funniest things was on the first Yes shows I did in America; we walked on and the audience used to throw spliffs on the stage – it's a slight exaggeration, but it felt like you were knee-deep in them. I mentioned this in an interview for an American magazine where I said that I had never taken drugs in my life and had no intention of ever doing so, as life was such a great natural high if you allowed it to be so, and the journalist asked me what my poison was and I replied, 'Drink, mainly beer, but spirits too.' From that moment, I'd arrive onstage to find cans and cans of alcohol piled up high by the side of the stage near my keyboards. If I'd replied 'drugs', I wouldn't be here now.

We've talked about the fact that I do everything to excess. I wouldn't have been content just to smoke the odd joint, I'd have taken copious amounts of everything. It would have killed me. I knew that and so I kept away.

Just as well I did.

Drugs would have been experienced to total excess, just like the drink, cigarettes, cars, my hair and the wives . . . although a drug habit would possibly have been less expensive than the wives.

Now to the part you've been racing through this chapter to get to.

Flatulence.

The problem was, for myself, and it has to be said for most bands at the time, with a predilection for curry, alcohol and on-going dubious health issues, flatulence was a very prominent feature of my daily life.

177

Not all the time, don't get me wrong.

Like not when I was sleeping, for example.

I don't think.

I had 'form' as they say, I'd got 'previous'. All of my band had severe flatulence problems. It's not uncommon among musicians. It's probably a combination of bad diet, bad lifestyles, beer, lack of fitness generally. One time in America with the English Rock Ensemble, everyone except me (for a change) had disgraceful flatulence. This American woman came in to interview me in the dressing room after a show and she could hardly get a word in for all the farting from the band. It was an art form for them. Carefully posed positions were very important. Standing on a chair and pre-empting what was to follow with 'Get a load of this one, chaps' was routine. Worse still, they had odour. She was disgusted and wasn't backwards in coming forwards in complaining. I tried in vain to conduct a serious interview while the rest of the band farted, gave marks out of ten for each effort on a whiteboard, and laughed uncontrollably. Eventually, she gave up and left in disgust. I could hardly disapprove because I was often the worst culprit, but I didn't fancy smelling their arses for the remainder of the evening, so I went to bed. When the article came out, she'd written: 'I accept they are phenomenal musicians and the show was undeniably tremendous, but they are not the kind of people I'd like to spend time with. The stench in the dressing room within minutes of coming off stage was not something I would inflict upon my worst enemy.'

And I fully expect that after I left the band that night, they continued their flatulence competition long into the early hours. But under no circumstances was I going to hang around and see who won.

'I'VE GOT CHE GUEVARA IN THE SHED'

I had always wanted to travel to Cuba. I wanted to go for one reason and one reason only: the music. The regime there had effectively, and in several ways quite rightly too, isolated Cuba from many aspects of the modern world for decades, but what that meant to me was that the music had not been 'bastardised', infected by outside influence. To a musician like me, that offered a musical culture with a purity that was very enticing. I'd been to Eastern Europe before the Wall came down, as you know, and to South Africa during the apartheid years, where I got into all sorts of trouble because I'd worked with black choirs and musicians . . . but that's another story . . .

I have, indeed, collected quite a few air miles on my jaunts around the world, but Cuba was always just out of reach. Obviously, it was politically problematic but nonetheless I had tried and tried and tried, year after year after year, to no avail. The closest I'd got was that a Cuban lawyer friend in Tenerife had persevered very hard for several years, but even he had no luck.

There were people who had managed to get down there. John Lennon was one of those musicians and there's even a monument to him in one of the parks – Lennon became quite a hero to the Cuban people and Castro ordered the monument to be created. Then, of course, there were smaller bands and lower-profile acts who'd gone there and played jazz places and festivals. But our band and show was a big concern and it wasn't happening. It could have been worse – American bands were just banned outright.

Then, in about 2006, I met a Swiss-Italian called Riki Braga who came to a show I was doing in Switzerland and afterwards he asked to talk to me about doing a charity show. Now, I get dozens and dozens of such requests, so it can be very hard to give them all the attention they deserve, but he seemed very nice so I asked him to tell me more. He explained that he and a friend were raising funds for a children's cancer hospital, and he went into great detail about what a brilliant charity it was and how hard they worked for these sick kids.

'Where is it in Switzerland?' I asked.

'It's in Cuba,' he replied.

'Well, unfortunately, that's just knocked it on the head because I can't get in there to play – been trying for years.'

'I can get you in.'

'Really? How?'

'There is authorisation from the government.'

Now I was starting to get palpitations.

'Are you serious?' Then reality hit home. 'Well, that sounds good but as soon as they look into my background we will be finished. Even though I am aware of Castro, Che Guevara and Cuban history and fully understand their situation, my personal politics will not be popular – I am a fully paid-up card-carrying member of the British Conservative Party. Also, my fiancée is a journalist from the West. So I can't see one of the last remaining communist countries in the world opening their doors to me.'

He listened to me and then said, 'Rick, you have already been cleared to play there.'

Now this was serious.

'What? Who by?'

'By Fidel Castro himself.'

'You're having me on.'

He wasn't.

I was so excited that I could hardly sleep. I was later introduced to the man who ran the fund raising for the hospital and was very impressed. Adding that charity to the chance to play in Cuba was just perfect.

Once I'd calmed down, the practicalities of playing there reared their ugly head. Logistically, the problems were colossal. For a start, as it was a charity show there was no funding available, obviously. The cost of getting myself, the band and all our extensive gear down to Cuba was *astronomical*. So we figured out that if we planned our route carefully and flew back via a couple of shows in Mexico and Costa Rica, that would help to part-finance these substantial expenses. Although I'd already been cleared, the immigration paperwork was a nightmare because there were few real precedents for bands going to Cuba on this scale so no forms actually existed, and the process was fraught with problems. But we eventually got the rubber stamp in all the right places. A caveat was that although we could get the gear to Cuba easily enough, the planes flying out of Cuba back to Mexico were not big enough to transport our equipment so we weren't even sure how we were going to get our stuff to the next port of call after the shows in Cuba. I have to say I didn't really care if I was left heavily out of pocket and without my gear – like with *King Arthur on Ice* I was at 9.8 on the 'Don't-Give-a-Toss-Meter'. The most important thing was to make it work because I wanted *so* much to go to Cuba.

Some months later, as the plane touched down in Cuba, I was like a little boy in a sweet shop, literally salivating at the prospect of hearing all this amazing music. I was there for ten days and went to forty-one concerts. Some of these concerts had been specially arranged for us to see, which was wonderful; others were just tiny local venues that we found and joined in. The music that I heard in those ten days . . . wow. Some of the players were indescribably good. I saw the best acoustic guitar player I have ever had the pleasure to witness, for example . . . brilliant.

The people were simply fabulous and nothing was too much trouble for them: we were treated magnificently. The most high-profile events were the two shows we were doing at the Karl Marx Theatre, which holds 6,000 people, and an open-air gig in Havana itself. It was quite daunting in a way, because although we had our own gear we had no idea what sort of PAs or house equipment we might find. Yet we were delighted to find everything was first class: my crew were ecstatic because they were given absolutely super stuff to work with.

Of course, this was Cuba, so it wasn't all plain sailing. A lovely lady called Yvette and a gentleman called Harrison – both very senior government officials – were assigned to 'accompany' us everywhere, just like in Poland, Moscow and in Paraguay; pretty soon I realised that they were actually just keeping an eye on my missus Rachel and me. At first Yvette and Harrison were a little apprehensive, but within a couple of days it obviously became clear that all our entourage were there because we wanted to sample Cuban culture and life, that our motives were pure. Then they relaxed and we got on famously.

One night Yvette came to our hotel and said, 'Rick, Fidel Castro is speaking tonight and you and Rachel will be our special guests.' We headed off to the Karl Marx Theatre and sat down in the front row of the balcony among thousands of people. It was exactly like you'd imagine, a real-life snippet from a movie: Castro walked onstage, flanked by rows of military men, war heroes and senior soldiers everywhere. The atmosphere was absolutely electric as Castro rose to approach the microphone.

He spoke for four hours.

With no notes.

Yvette translated for Rachel and myself as he spoke. He was impassioned, intellectual, compelling – it was a truly amazing experience. Interestingly, it wasn't what I thought I was going to hear, either. It wasn't some huge anti-Western rhetoric or rant. It was all about how we need to look after the world and how we need to understand how we are wasting energy and wasting food and, understandably, he asked why the American government didn't seem to be aware of this. He even said he thought American people understood the problem: that Cuba liked American people, but the US government was a different matter.

You would think that four hours of a speech would be boring, tiring, dull, but I have to tell you that it was incredible.

But it was about to get far more incredible.

After Castro finished, the people were chanting his name and there was still a phenomenal atmosphere in the huge theatre, almost like that of a rock concert which has the audience baying for more. Yvette was approached by some government officials and then she turned to talk to me.

'Fidel would like to meet you, Rick.'

We were then escorted down a side aisle in the opposite direction to the now-departing audience, and through a door which led into the back of the venue. It was interesting to note that there was little or no security. No armed guards or anything like that. I naturally thought I'd just line up with several hundred other people, shake Castro's hand as he walked past and, if I was lucky, say 'Hello.'

How wrong could I be? There was just myself and Rachel, my tour manager Paul Silveira and Riki Braga. We spoke for almost forty minutes, face to face, through his translator.

I will always remember him looking me straight in the eye while the translator said, 'Fidel knows you are a humanitarian

183

and wants you to know that that is what he is too. It is important to care about each other. Always remember that.' He spoke
about how he worried about people starving and how he had
heard I was a good man who cared about such things. It was
really the most remarkable situation to find myself in, not just
meeting him but talking to him and, even more fantastic, he
knew certain things about me. When our chat came to a close,
I said what a privilege it had been to meet him and, by way of
a closing comment, asked him when he was next doing a speech.
He was known for just deciding to hold public speeches spon-
taneously, unplanned, sometimes at very short notice.

'Tomorrow night, here.'

Oh bugger.

I was supposed to be playing two shows here tomorrow
night.

Yvette knew exactly what I was thinking and hurried and hushed
conversations were held in Cuban Spanish. Castro listened
intently, then leaned right in by me. I was, not intimidated, but
in awe; even though he is a very slight man these days he had
such a huge presence and I didn't know how he was going to
react. Up close, his face was very angular and imposing and he
is much taller than he looks on TV.

He smiled and then spoke to his translator.

'Fidel says you will play here tomorrow night. He will find
another venue at which to speak.' The translator continued, on
Fidel's behalf: 'Because I am making a speech, unfortunately I
will not be attending the concert but many of my government
officials, especially the cultural minister, are going to be there.'

And, with that, he left.

Do you know, even though I had gone to Cuba to raise funds
for a children's cancer hospital and treatment centre, I was
appalled to find out that I got the most abysmal press in
America. I didn't care about what they said on a professional

level, I'm used to that, but it disgusted me that they were so vicious about a trip with such good intentions. Not one single American journalist bothered to ask me about the hospital or the children, not one. All they cared about was making scathing attacks on this musician who had dared to mix with Cubans and Castro. One even wrote I only went there deliberately to support the communist regime. As an ardent Thatcherite, they obviously hadn't done their homework! I was so disgusted, it was absolutely outrageous and I thought, *I'm not having this*, so I posted a big piece on my rwcc.com website. I explained that the hospital itself was absolutely fantastic – in cancer treatment they seemed light years ahead of anywhere in the Western world. They can cure cancers or slow down cancers that are terminal here – it was quite phenomenal. We met the most wonderful kids and went to their parties and played with them. It was so pure and so enriching; yet all the American writers could do was criticise.

Almost everything the Western world tells us about Cuba is wrong. The general public are fed what they are fed, but it is wrong. The truth of the matter is that Cuba is truly the jewel of the Caribbean, just a stone's throw from the American coast, and it *pisses* the Western world off that they cannot control it.

However, that does not dilute one bit the amazing time I had in Cuba. After we'd played those shows, we were faced with the seemingly insurmountable problem of getting our gear out of the country. As I mentioned, the planes flying out of Cuba could not accommodate our gear so, remarkably, Castro intervened and had wooden cases custom-made by expert furniture makers to be an exact fit – they looked like the world's most expensive coffins! He even had a carpet manufacturer make exact wraps for inside the cases and around the instruments. People worked twenty-four hours a day through the night to make them for us, as his gesture of thanks to us for going to Cuba. Remarkable.

185

And, yes, I've got Che Guevara in the shed, you know. Well, not exactly all of him, but a small part. Here's how.

During my stay there, I'd been taken to the memorial for Che Guevara in the north of the island. His remains had been found in Bolivia where he was killed, brought back to Cuba and put into a casket in this grave. It was so interesting.

Fast-forward to leaving Cuba with all our hand-made wooden cases ready to head for the airport; Yvette came over to me and said, 'I have a present for you. It's from Fidel, but you must hide it.'

She quickly gave me a Tupperware box inside which was some white-looking earth. I asked what it was and Yvette told me it was some of the earth that they found Che Guevara's remains in.

'Fidel wants you to have it as a reminder. He has the other half.'

I hid the Tupperware container in one of the keyboard trunks they'd made. When I got home, the safest place I could think of to put it initially was in my shed – after all, no one would think twice about some earth in a garden shed (it is now safely locked away in my lawyer's safe). One day I will get a small sample framed with the picture of myself with Castro and give the rest to a museum.

In the meantime, it's safe. As long as I don't tell anyone . . .

'HELLO, RICK,
I'M RONNIE BIGGS'

My love of football is well known. I've been a director of Brentford, chairman of Camberley Town, a part-owner of Philadelphia Fury in the US and have also followed Man City avidly for years. So when you get a call to play in Brazil – regardless of how difficult it might be to get bloody visas – you always sit up and listen. I've explained how difficult it is to actually handle the paperwork, so let me tell you now about what can actually happen when you finally get through customs.

From a financial point of view, in the mid-1970s there was little point in going to Brazil at all. My records were sold down there for years, but I had absolutely no idea how many copies were being shifted and I certainly didn't expect to see a royalty statement. There were stories about smaller bands venturing there and never being paid so it was generally considered a no-go area. Not for me.

One morning, Deal-a-Day Lane got a call from an agent by the name of Albert Koski. He wanted me and the band to go down to Brazil to play 'some big shows', performing *Journey to the Centre of the Earth* and *King Arthur*, which were both hugely popular, with a symphony orchestra. Deal-a-Day was dead set against it.

'Why? Rio de Janeiro, São Paulo, Copacabana Beach – it sounds great!'

'You'll never get paid, Rick, no one does. Plus, they haven't got any suitable equipment down there and, let's face it, you aren't exactly putting on the most simple show, so there'd be massive hidden costs. It's just all too risky. We can't do it.'

'Oh, but I really fancy this.'

'Absolutely not.'

As soon as Deal-a-Day had left the room, I picked up the phone and called my friend Chris Welch at *Melody Maker*. I told him, 'Guess what? I'm going to Brazil . . .'

They printed a big news-piece story in the very next issue.

Deal-a-Day was not pleased.

'Did they print it? I only mentioned it in passing to him over a pint . . .' I lied, weakly.

Deal-a-Day angrily informed me that since *Melody Maker* had run the piece the phone had been ringing off the hook with enquiries and both the British and Brazilian press were all over it. Eventually, with a large resigned sigh, he said, 'All right, all right, on your head be it . . . let's go to Brazil.'

The dates were arranged to follow on from some US shows, to keep the costs to a minimum. As we sat on the plane heading out of New York for Rio, we genuinely had absolutely no idea of what awaited us: how many fans – if any, what sort of press interest, we knew nothing. I'd flown ahead of the band to do a day of press interviews, and the whole series of shows was being sponsored by a company called El Globo, which was an enormous media corporation.

On the plane next to me was Funky Fat Fred, the most wonderful but quite simply the worst tour manager in the world. Let me finally introduce him fully and tell you a few stories, before we get on to the Brazilian trip proper.

I loved Funky Fat Fred – he was just dreadful at his job. For example, a tour manager's first job of the day is to get everybody up in the morning and ready to go; the problem was, Fred was always the last man up; he regularly got the 'golden blanket' award. Fred never ever heard his early morning call, so we used to take it in turns to put calls into ourselves and then go to Fred's room with a spare key to wake him up in person. Once we had woken him up, just to keep him happy we'd all go back to bed again so he could then get us up and feel he was doing his job. He would invariably send us to the wrong airports, the wrong hotels, the wrong venues and even on one occasion the wrong country. But I wouldn't have swapped Fred for the world. He had been a steward on the *Canberra* among many other jobs and he was worldly-wise, even if he didn't ever really seem to know exactly where in the world he was. Roger Newell, my bass player, often did the actual job of tour managing and when Fred was holding court, telling us upcoming plans, it was nothing short of hilarious.

'Right, lads, we've got a ten o'clock start tomorrow,' Fred would say.

'Nine o'clock,' Roger would interject.

'Then we're off to JFK . . .'

'Newark, Fred . . .'

'. . . in two cars . . .'

'Three, Fred.'

'. . . so the luggage needs to be ready for eight o'clock.'

'Seven.'

It was quality entertainment for the rest of us. We used to sit there with our drinks listening to it and loving every minute, regardless of the consequences for the tour schedule. It was such fun.

Fred had a very odd line in girlfriends. Without putting too fine a point on it – and I'm not even sure the PC Brigade will let me tell this story but here goes – there was always something drastically wrong with them. Not their personalities, all of them were very lovely girls. But there was always something wrong with them and I'm not just talking about a minor ailment. Recalling some of his female company over the years, there was one with a leg missing, another who appeared to have an extra ear, there was a bald one who suffered from alopecia which also reminds me of the one who had more facial hair than a member of ZZ Top. I don't know if these girls were drawn to Funky Fat Fred or if he was drawn to them, but either way we never knew what to expect when he started seeing a new woman.

One particular night in America, Funky Fat Fred seemed to have had a change of luck. We were at a club in the basement of the hotel we were staying at in Chicago and the whole band was in a mischievous mood. The bouncers told Hodgy (my tuned percussionist) off for not dressing formally enough, ordering him to 'Come back when you are wearing a tie,' which he did. Except that was all he was wearing, stark bollock naked except for this little grey tie. Some people found that quite funny; the bouncers didn't, as I remember.

The police were very good about it.

Anyway, we'd all come back from the show and there was no sign of Fred. Someone asked me to give him a knock on the way past his room and check he was all right – like Chris Squire, he could fall asleep at any given moment. So I knocked on his hotel room door and noticed it was slightly ajar. I walked in quietly and there, lying on the bed completely naked, was a gorgeous-looking blonde. Quite stunning! Fred was there too, and they were obviously 'together'.

I've got to be honest, I did make a very quick count: two arms, two legs, two ears, two eyes, single nose, no beard . . . all seemed present and correct with this blonde beauty. It seems harsh, but with Fred's women you did have to do the odd limb count.

'Oh, sorry, Fred, just checking you're OK,' I apologised.

'All right, Rick,' said Fred, nonchalantly. 'We're good, thanks. This is Sue by the way.'

I smiled in her direction, and she smiled back at me.

Another surprise: she appeared to have her own teeth as well!

'I'll see you downstairs in a little while.'

Shocked, I walked back down to the club where the band were propping themselves up with several glasses of alcoholic beverages. (Have you noticed how bands never sit at tables, they always sit up at the bar?) Anyway, I joined the guys and one of them said, 'You all right, Rick? You look like you've had a shock.'

'I'm fine, thanks, but not as fine as Fred. He's only got himself an absolute stunner in his room: blonde, slim and, last I saw, naked.'

'Really?' came the sceptical reply. 'Has she got any limbs missing?'

'All present and correct, I counted 'em myself.'

'Really? You sure? Two noses?'

'No.'

'Six fingers on each hand?'

'No.'

'Four tits and six nipples?'

'No, honestly, she was gorgeous, and they're coming down in a minute so you'll see for yourself.'

Sure enough, about ten minutes later, Fred walks in the bar with this Amazonian blonde, tall, leggy, elegant and very beautiful. The band's jaws dropped. You could see them all counting, *Two arms, two legs, two . . .*

Fred knew what we were thinking and he'd got the biggest grin across his face. He brought this girl over and introduced her to us all and we said hello to her.

She looked back at us and very gently said, 'It'th luthvely thoo thee you all.'

As cool as you like, Fred leaned over in front of her and said, 'Cleft palate.'

Fred may have been a crap tour manager but he was just wonderful, absolutely wonderful. He's still knocking about somewhere, he's like the Del Boy Trotter of Buckinghamshire. I loved him to bits.

Anyway, back to Brazil: Fred was with me on this flight down to Rio to 'chaperone' me. We were flying Varig Airlines and were sitting in first class and, naturally, we both sank a few on the way there. As we came in to land, Fred went a bit quiet. I looked out the window and said, 'Fred, something's going on here . . .'

There were thousands of people at the airport, on parapets, the various terminal building roofs, the runway, the parking lots, everywhere. The best way I could describe it is like the pictures I saw of when the Beatles first arrived in New York.

'I know, Rick. Football, I suspect – they love their football down here. It must be the national team arriving.'

Wrong.

The intercom on the plane crackled to life. 'Would all passengers please remain in their seats until Mr Wakeman has safely disembarked the aeroplane.'

The stewardess came over to our seats and told us that special arrangements had been made for our safety and would we please accompany her to the front exit door of the plane?

When they opened the doors, there was pandemonium. Later reports put the crowd at 100,000 people. There was a parade of sleek black limos right next to the side of the plane, each with two or three besuited security men in dark glasses standing by an open door, a veritable cavalcade waiting for Funky Fat Fred and myself.

We were guided into the nearest limo and as soon as we got in a security man asked us for our passports and papers. We didn't go anywhere near customs or passport control this time, but instead were whisked straight out of a side exit to the airport and headed off to Rio. Even more insanely, when we got close to Copacabana Beach the streets were lined with even more people, shouting, holding up my records, waving banners and flags. It was pure madness. I will own up to loving every minute of it. I mean, who wouldn't?

It turned out that El Globo, the media company backing the whole venture, had a virtual monopoly on the newspapers and radio and TV, and so had been plugging the events almost ceaselessly for weeks. I also learned that they'd invited other big bands from Europe to play there, but no one would go. So it was one of the most anticipated music shows in Brazil for years. Then someone showed me the equivalent of the *Melody Maker* charts and my records were at numbers 1, 2, 3, 4 and 5. The biggest and best symphony orchestra and choir had been confirmed for the show as well, so this was going to be about as big as it got.

As we drove through the city I enquired about the indoor venue we'd be playing and what it was like, if the capacity was known and so on.

'It's at least 35,000 at each show each night, Rick. You are playing two shows a night for six days. They all sold out months ago.'

OK, so now I knew that we did have a following in Brazil.

We pulled up at the hotel and there was an armed guard waiting to escort us from the limo into the foyer, again for safety reasons. When we got to our rooms there was an armed guard posted outside each door and we were not allowed to leave under any circumstances. Although I've played in some fairly popular bands, I've never really considered myself a pop star and I certainly haven't felt my life has been impeded in the way that big pop stars experience such things. But in Brazil I could understand some of these problems. As you know from my antics in Poland and Moscow I'm pretty adept at slinking off, but in Brazil I just couldn't go anywhere without being escorted or without detailed military planning. My minders had their reasons, though, as I would later find out. If I wanted to go to the pool, they would say, 'When, exactly? And for how long? And who is going with you? And who might meet up with you while you are there?' They even cleared certain areas of the pool. And when they asked us these questions, it always sounded so comical when I'd reply, 'Well, I might meet Deal-a-Day or Funky Fat Fred, if he isn't too pissed.'

Let's take a quick diversion to the pool before I continue my tale. It was like a United Nations mission just getting to a sunlounger. Finally, on one afternoon I made it to the pool and was very much enjoying relaxing in the sun and sampling the local alcohol.

Suddenly this very English voice says to me, 'Hello, Rick, how's London?'

It was Ronnie Biggs.

There, in a nutshell, is one of the very odd aspects of being a public face, of so-called celebrity – or perhaps notoriety, I should say in my case. People who are complete strangers know you and, if they are equally high-profile, you know them. Yet actually you don't know each other at all, you are indeed complete strangers. It's a forced intimacy that is really quite odd. Sometimes if it's a fellow musician or, in my younger days, a very beautiful actress, then it's very handy. But when it's Ronnie Biggs, it's really rather peculiar.

'Hello, Ronnie,' I said jovially.

'How you doing? Can I join you for a beer?'

This trip was rapidly becoming something like a surreal dream. There I was, sitting by a pool in Brazil, visibly armed security guards watching my every move, supping on a beer with Ronnie Biggs, Great Train Robber and escaped prisoner! We talked about jolly old England, football, the government, all sorts. Then I said, 'Do you miss England, Ronnie?'

Just as the words left my beer-drenched lips, an absolutely

stunning Brazilian woman sauntered past us wearing a thong bikini and with her bosom heaving and glinting in the heat of the glorious sun.

I looked at Ronnie, Ronnie looked at me, we both looked at the girl and he said, 'Yeah! Of course!'

We chatted some more and he revealed that he was really looking forward to the shows. I said if there was anything I could do to help re tickets etc. to let me know. Ronnie smiled and said, 'Well, actually, Ricky, I have got a few friends it would be nice to look after . . .' and as he spoke he pointed at some other sunloungers which were occupied by some 'friends'. All English, mostly Londoners and obviously not on holiday. I burst out laughing, and so did all the guys.

Over the next few days, we chatted regularly. He spoke about music, sport, even the Great Train Robbery on occasion. He was a very articulate man and very interesting and it was fascinating talking to him. It reminded me of a bygone age when entertainers, police and criminals all dovetailed together. It still goes on to a certain extent, of course it does, but back then there was a certain interlinked dynamic between the underworld, the showbiz world and the legal world.

Anyway, one day Ronnie asked me if I would do him a favour. He'd recently divorced from his wife and she was now living in Australia. Ronnie asked if it was possible that the next time I played Down Under I could deliver her one of my albums. I said, 'Of course!' And some months later, I did exactly that . . .

The funny thing was that the police and Special Branch must have been watching at some point, because a few days after I landed back in Blighty I got a visit. Two men asked me what I was doing in Australia and when I said 'on tour' they replied, 'And did you give anything to anybody?' That was when I cottoned on that they had obviously been conducting surveillance on Ronnie's wife.

I said, 'I'm a musician. I was fourteen when the Great Train Robbery took place – do you think I took a day off school to help them out and hid the money in my satchel or something?' To be fair, they laughed. They asked me why I had been seen meeting Ronnie Biggs's ex-wife.

'Because I'd been asked to deliver a copy of *The Six Wives of Henry VIII* in person.'

They laughed some more and left.

Back in my suite at the top of the Rio hotel, there were so many rooms it was hilarious. It was bigger than my house . . . which was pretty big itself. It was absolutely barking, it truly felt like a Beatles experience.

When it came to the shows we had to be smuggled out, do the soundcheck under tight security and then be smuggled back to the hotel. The orchestra down in Brazil was absolutely sublime. One of the great things about that mini-tour is that we still hold all of the indoor records for those places. We were doing 35,000 a night but that level of capacity was clearly so dangerous that, fairly soon afterwards, limits were put on of around 18,000. So no one can ever come close to our crowd figures!

The unattached members of the band were also having a whale of a time, and found themselves 'attached' very quickly and very easily. I distinctly remember opening a linen cupboard in the hotel only to find one of the band in flagrante with a Brazilian woman I'd never seen before. And all he said, as cool as you like, was, 'I'm looking for a clean towel, Rick, and this kind young chambermaid is helping me.'

'Well, she won't find a towel where she's looking,' I said.

During the course of those few days, I absolutely fell in love with Brazil and its people. They were so warm – they didn't always have much but they couldn't give you enough. They smiled and they loved music. Most restaurants had tambourines or small instruments on the tables and when the house band started playing everybody just joined in. They don't walk anywhere, they just seem to dance. The food was fantastic, the people were just so happy and they were so pleased that we were down there. We were having the most wonderful time.

But just when we thought it couldn't get any more bizarre, we had a message one day saying that a very important 'someone' had come to see me. Security came up to my room and I was escorted in silence in a private elevator downstairs. I was taken to a small room and when I walked in, there, sitting in front of me, was one of the most famous Brazilian international superstar footballers of all time, Rivelino.

I didn't know what to say, I was so shocked. The Brazilians are all football nuts so it was a great privilege to even meet him. The whole of Copacabana Beach was filled with goal posts and I saw some of the greatest football in my life played on that sand. If there was a spare bit of ground they'd be kicking around a ball . . . or dancing, or singing or playing.

He'd brought a translator with him and through this man he said he'd heard I liked football. I told him, 'Very much so.'

'I hear you have a football team with your band and your people,' he enquired.

'Well, we do have a kick-about now and then, for fun, yes.'

'Well, would you like to play a game while you are staying with us here in Brazil?'

'Yes, that would be fantastic!'

At this point I was thinking we might sneak out into the hotel car park and have a ten-minute knockabout.

'I will arrange it all,' he said, via this translator. 'We will contact all the press and work with the stadium to organise the match . . .'

OK, so this wasn't going to be in the car park outside, then . . .

'. . . And I will get a team from the press together for the match at Fluminense Stadium.'

This was the Brazilian equivalent of playing at Old Trafford.

He explained that the match would have to be played close to midnight as otherwise the heat would simply be too much for us Brits. With that, he made his way out. I could hardly believe it, bearing in mind that I was just thrilled to meet the man himself. The day before, they asked us if there was anything we'd like and we said it would be really nice if could get a team strip. No problem. Then I asked if we could go to the ground in a proper team coach, which again they said was no problem. Come the evening of the match, we were half pissed by the time the coach arrived, having a fantastic time.

I figured that, playing so late at night and being a bunch of British rock-and-rollers versus a team made up of the media, it would be a quiet bit of fun, like one of those games played behind closed doors.

On our team coach was a man called Roberto from El Globo. As the coach weaved its way through the thronging crowds of Rio, I chatted with him and asked him why there were so many people out late at night. The place was swarming.

'Oh, they are going to a football match.'

These Brazilians, eh? They love their bloody football.

'Really? Brilliant, who's playing?'

'Why, you are, Rick.'

The coach pulled up at the stadium and there were 30,000 people there, a capacity sell-out.

At eleven o'clock at night.

It was nuts.

Then we caught sight of the numerous TV crews who were all covering the game live from pretty much every angle. By now, nothing surprised me.

We went out there and had an amazing time. The press had some really useful players – I think some of them had even played professionally at a high level with the glittering Brazilian leagues.

We had a couple of tasty players too – one guy called Toby had even had a trial for Carlisle (or maybe he had been on trial in Carlisle, it was one way or the other anyway).

We lost 4–2 but I never actually got to hear the final whistle. With about ten minutes to go, a Jeep suddenly roared onto the middle of the pitch. Then these huge security men leapt out and grabbed me, lifted me off the ground and virtually threw me into the back, at which point the Jeep thundered off the grass and drove off out of the stadium.

'What on earth is going on?' I asked, not unreasonably.

'We've just had a kidnap threat against you.'

I was safely back in the hotel in what seemed like minutes. Kidnap or no kidnap, I didn't care, I'd had the time of my life.

Oh, and in case you were wondering, we did get paid.

Well, only a little bit, but no one was counting.

Mervyn Conn would have been proud.

EPILOGUE

Remember Igor, my friend from Russian security who helped me smuggle two illegal military uniforms and $2,000 out of Russia? Well, fifteen years later I was at Heathrow Airport when I saw a man in a queue whom I swore I knew. I caught his eye and he walked over with a huge grin on his face.

It was Igor.

After we'd said hello, I asked, 'What on earth are you doing here?'

'Well, my country is changed now, the Wall has come down and everything is different. My job is no longer existing, so I work in senior position for government airline to seek out new airports to operate from and to look for new routes that might be possible for Russian people.'

'Fantastic, Igor, what a job!' I enthused. 'What sort of places are you researching?'

'I just back from Bermuda and now I fly to Barbados. No good for airline, but for me, is good,' he said with a smile. 'And you? What have you been doing?'

'Oh, crikey, well . . .'

My mind filled with thoughts of Paraguay, Deal-a-Day, Portugal, heart attacks, cars, breeze-blocks, Snow White, Rupert the Bear, Funky Fat Fred, vintage champagne, Peter Sellers, my nan and Che Guevara . . .

'Oh, all sorts, Igor, all sorts.'

We chatted for a few more minutes and then Igor's expression turned a little serious.

'Rick, can I ask you a question?'

'Anything, Igor.'

'Did you know how much trouble you could have been in over those uniforms?'

'Yes, I did. Thank you again for all that.'

'And do you still have the uniforms, Rick?'

'Yes, I most certainly do.'

He explained that, ironically, since the Wall had come down and so many military jobs had become obsolete, the uniforms were now freely available at markets all over Russia.

'Is ten a penny now, Rick.'

I laughed and said, 'Igor, can I ask *you* a question?'

'Anything, Rick.'

'Do you still have the vinyl records I sent?'

'Of course, of course.'

'Even The Yes?'

'Even The Yes. The vinyl, they came to me very fast and I thank you, Rick.'

'Well, since CDs came in, they're ten a penny too.'

Is good.

ACKNOWLEDGEMENTS

It is actually impossible to name everybody who has contributed to my life in one way or another, and therefore in turn have contributed to many of the adventures I relate in this book, but a few do deserve a special mention, as without them I may well have walked through completely different doors in the music and entertainment industry.

Firstly, two men, (both sadly no longer with us). Oscar Beuselinck was the greatest showbiz lawyer you could possibly wish for and he certainly influenced and helped me greately as indeed did David Moss, who was my accountant for fifteen years up until the mid-eighties. David fought valiantly throughout this period to inject some financial sense into my head, but eventually admitted defeat!

Brian 'Deal-a-Day' Lane, was the epitome of rock 'n' roll management and I could quite easily write a book on him alone, but he probaby wouldn't be happy with some of the chapters!

Jerry Moss and the brothers Ahmet and Nessui Ertegun were the greatest bossesof A&M records and WEA respectively and the likes of which will never be seen again.

On the Grumpy side of things, I really must acknowledge my

great friend Stuart Pebble, who was the genius behind the *Grumpy Old Men* television series.

I could probably fill this book with names of people that perhaps I should have acknowledged, but if I listed them all, then it wouldn't leave any room for the stories that many of them played their part in, and so, if you are somebody reading this that feels they should be included in the acknowledgements . . . then I acknowledge you!

ILLUSTRATION CREDITS

Section 1

Rick at the Festival Hall, 1974 © Mirrorpix
The Strawbs, 1970 © Michael Ochs Archives /Gettyimages
Rick portrait © GEMS/Redferns
English rock ensemble © GEMS/Redferns
Yes, 1976 (top left) © GAB Archives/Redferns
NME front cover, 1974 courtesy *New Musical Express*
King Arthur on Ice concerts © Jonathan Player/Rex Features
Lisztomania © The Ronald Grant Archive
Lisztomania © Everett Collection/Rex Features
Rick and horse © Michael Putland/Retna
The cast of *King Arthur on Ice* © Mirrorpix
Rick in No Earthly Connection cape © Andrew Putler/Redferns

Section 2

Rick playing chess © Neal Preston/Corbis
At the keyboards: top © Ian Dickson/Redferns, middle © Adam
Pensotti/Rex Features, bottom © Fin Costello/Redferns

Rick and Eric Sykes © Jules Annan/Retna
Rick on a tractor © Keith Butler/Rex Features
Yes © Fotex Agentur GMBH/Redferns
Sydney Entertainment Centre © Bob King/Redferns
Rick in a submarine © David Corio
Yes, 2004 © Mick Hutson/Redferns

Photographs not listed are from the author's personal collection.

While every effort has been made to trace the owners of copyright material reproduced herein, the publishers would like to apologise for any omissions and will be pleased to incorporate missing acknowledgements in any future editions.

INDEX

A NOTE ON THE AUTHORS

Rick Wakeman is the most gifted keyboard player of his generation, as at home onstage at a rock concert as in the organ loft of a great cathedral. As keyboard player for the 70s super-group Yes his extraordinary live tours and multimillion-selling albums are legendary. He has also appeared on *Top Gear* achieving a lamentable lap time of 1.55.26.

Martin Roach, who collaborated with Rick Wakeman on this book, is a five-time *Sunday Times* best-selling author who has written more than a hundred books on music, entertainment and youth culture.